Francis Murray of Chislehurst

Jean M Pailing

Published by: Jean M Pailing
9 Adcock Walk
Orpington
Kent BR6 9SY
Great Britain

Printed by Cantate Bishops, Orpington, Kent (01689 821105)

ISBN 0-9542645-0-9

Contents

Illustrations

Foreword

In some respects there was nothing unique about Canon F.H. Murray's incumbency of St Nicholas', Chislehurst, instituting a vigorous and dignified system of worship after the slovenliness and neglect which had become so common in the previous hundred years or so; and bolstering the new situation with a group of clergy bound together by strict spiritual discipline, as with the Society of the Holy Cross. At the same time he organised numerous schemes to help alleviate the consequences of the appalling poverty prevalent among working class people.

All of this could usually be found in any large town from the middle of the nineteenth century. The Vicar under whom I grew up began as a curate at St John the Divine, Chatham, in the early 1900s and he used to tell us what life was like in the parish in those days. There were the well-to-do people who sat in padded pews in the middle of the church, and there were those who lived in dingy terraced houses, many of whom were too poor and shabby to attend the Parish Church, so they were provided with the Mission Church of St Martin as their place of worship.

There were three or four nuns who worked in the parish, members of the Order of the Sisters of Bethany. There were social clubs, savings clubs, clothing clubs, etc., all organized by the three curates and the sisters. And the previous Rector had revolutionized the worship, introducing daily services, with Evensong sung on three weekdays every week.

Where Chislehurst differed from other places during Canon Murray's long incumbency was in its aristocratic set-up, with a rigid distinction between the gentry and the working classes. Social activities were organised for the poor, but nearly always as an act of condescension from their superiors. I can recall one of our lecturers at the Theological College, speaking about the Victorian heyday of the Church of England, saying that if the workers had been paid properly, they would have been able to look after themselves when they were ill, and would not have wanted soup brought to them by servants from the Rector's lady wife.

We could say that Canon Murray and his like alleviated society's sickness, but took no steps to cure it. On that score they can be criticized, but not condemned.

It was left to the next generation to go all-out to get justice and decent treatment for the ordinary workers, culminating in the legislation of the Labour government following its landslide victory in the 1945 General Election. And the ironical thing is that the Church of England's foremost advocate of social reform was himself from an out-and-out aristocratic background, the famous William Temple, who had lived most of his life in palaces! His father was Bishop of Exeter when he was born, then he became Bishop of London and eventually Archbishop of Canterbury. William himself was Bishop of Manchester, then Archbishop of York, and finally Archbishop of Canterbury like his father. The tragedy was that William Temple died prematurely in 1944 after only two and a half years at Canterbury, so he didn't see the triumph of the social justice he had fought for. For the last five years of his time at Chislehurst, Canon Murray had Frederick Temple as his Diocesan.

While we may fairly criticize Canon Murray and his like without condemning them, have we anything to learn from them in the very different conditions of everyday life now? We certainly have! When they saw poverty and ignorance they did something about it, in accordance with their limited convictions. They fervently believed in the Church of England as the historic spiritual home of the majority of the nation, with a consequent duty to speak out when necessary on religious and moral issues.

That is what we lack nowadays. We are left floundering in a whirlpool of spiritual and moral possibilities. We need to recover the outlook and conviction of Canon Murray and his contemporaries, with Canterbury speaking for the nation, and incumbents for their locality.

RONALD D. SMITH
Bromley College
Bromley

January 2002

Acknowledgements

I am grateful to the staff of The British Library which I first used when in its original setting, and later in its glorious re-incarnation at St Pancras. The former afforded the unforgettable experience of working in Panizzi's domed Reading Room. Lambeth Palace Library must be one of the most speedy and efficient libraries in existence and the Guildhall Library is a treasure house of material relating to London. The Public Records Office at Kew, although vast in its collection of material, makes research very easy. Smaller libraries have provided friendly, personal service: Pusey House Library in Oxford, the Local Studies Library in Bromley, and the Kent Local Studies Centre at Maidstone. Gordon Knights of The Canterbury Press, Norwich, gave me permission to study the *Hymns Ancient and Modern* archive and I received valuable help from the archivists of Christ Church College, Oxford, and Harrow School. In the library of Keble College, Oxford, I studied the correspondence relating to the patronage of the Church of the Annunciation to the Blessed Virgin Mary.

The Rev. Michael Shields, a former Master General of the SSC, has lent a rare photograph of Charles Lowder while the Rev. Trevor Jones SSC, Vicar of St Peter's, London Docks, generously allowed me to spend a day going over related material.

My most comfortable research took place at the gracious home of Cdr Nigel Anderdon and the late Mrs Mavis Anderdon: I shall always treasure the memories of their hospitality and be grateful for the preliminary work that Mrs Anderdon had done on the family archives. The Curator of the Somerset County Cricket Club Museum supplied me with information on Francis Murray's son, Henry Murray-Anderdon.

At St Nicholas' Church there are many to thank: the Rev. John Allen for his enthusiastic encouragement way back in 1997 and his successor, the Rev. Christopher Walker, for his continuing support and interest. Peter Masson opened up the church archive and verified many snippets of information while John McDermott, the previous Headmaster of St Nicholas' School, allowed me a long perusal of the school Log Books and the Trustees' Minute Books. Last, but not least, the Parochial Church Council generously paid for the photographing and printing of pictures from the Anderdon collection.

I must thank also The Chislehurst Society for allowing me space in *The Cockpit* for advance publicity and I am enormously indebted to Roy Hopper in particular for feeding me with new material as it came to light and allowing me to benefit from his knowledge of Chislehurst's past.

Peter Street of Birkbeck College has my unfailing gratitude for a truly inspiring course of lectures on Religion and Society: this did a lot towards putting Francis Murray into a historical context. Hazel Davey and Jean Day together brought back interesting facts from the Isle of Man which put him into his early geographical setting.

In quite a different way I want to thank Georgina Collins who, when I have most needed it, has given me that precious commodity – time.

How can I thank sufficiently those members of my family who have so loyally borne me up in this enterprise: Marcus, Crispin, Rowena, and Caroline? Their suggested alterations, their observations, their kind interest have all been noted. The faults and inadequacies which remain are my responsibility.

Most importantly I am dedicating this book to my husband, James. A rare neurological condition has deprived him of the physical ability to pursue the academic interests which would have been his delight. With characteristic generosity he has encouraged me to go ahead and has patiently endured much on the matter of the Victorian Church. As ever, his confidence has been my strength.

Jean M. Pailing
January 2002

Preface

The turn of the century and then the centenary, in January 2001, of the death of Queen Victoria released a flood of literature on 'The Victorian Age'. This book is but a tiny contribution to that literature.

It examines the life and career of Francis Henry Murray, Rector of St Nicholas' Church, Chislehurst, Kent, from 1846 -1902. Except for a monograph by Nigel Yates in *Archaeologia Cantiana* no. 98 (1982) there has been no other study of Francis Murray. However, the indices to many books about nineteenth century developments in the Church of England yield references to him: he was perhaps not a national figure, but very nearly so.

This is more than just the life of Francis Murray. To understand him fully it is necessary to remind readers of the historical background to the controversial developments of the nineteenth century, for example the Oxford Movement and the Public Worship Regulation Act. I hope that readers will bear with me if they are familiar with the material in the history chapters and will find it helpful if they are not. On the other hand, there are some key clergy figures whom I have introduced without explanation feeling that they are too well-known to be described in detail: men such as John Keble and Edward Pusey.

Inevitably, much local detail has emerged and this will be of particular interest to the present-day residents of Chislehurst but, even without a local connection, readers will recognise that the essence of Chislehurst life was repeated all over England.

Explanation is required for the two initialisms which I have used. To a great extent I have referred to Francis Henry Murray as FHM: this seemed a useful and respectful device, and I think he would have approved. The Society of the Holy Cross is given as SSC: these are the initials of the original Latin title *Societas Sanctae Crucis*.

It has been a privilege to unearth the life-story of Francis Murray. He has accompanied me back into a world of high-minded people, dedicated to the pursuit of holiness. He has reminded me of the diversity of Victorian life and the Church's role in improving social welfare and he has demonstrated his technique of effecting change in a parish. Any antagonism he generated was managed with dignified authority. Like so many clergy of his time he devoted his life to just one place: Chislehurst and its churches are his enduring memorial.

Murray

- **John Murray**, **1st Duke of Atholl**, **1660 - 1724** = Lady Katherine Hamilton
  - Lord John, *killed at Malplaquet 1709*
  - Lord William, *Jacobite* (atteinted)
  - **James**, **2nd Duke of Atholl**, **1690 – 1764**, **m. Jean née Frederick**
    - **Charlotte**, **Baroness Strange**, ***only surviving child of 2nd Duke*** = **John**, **3rd Duke of Atholl**, **1729 - 1774**
      - John, 4th Duke of Atholl, 1755 - 1830
      - Ann Grant, d. 1844 = **Lord George**, ***fourth son***, **1761 – 1803**, ***Bishop of Saint Davids (shutter signalling)***
        - **George**, ***second son***, **1784 – 1860**, ***Bishop of Rochester*** = Lady Sarah Hay-Drummond, d. 1894
          - 1. Fanny Anderdon, d. 1850 = **Francis Henry Murray**, ***second son***, **1820 – 1902**, ***Rector of St Nicholas' Chistlehurst*** = 2. Mary Saunders, d. 1886
            - Henry Edward Murray-Anderdon, 1848 – 1922, *President of Somerset County Cricket Club*
            - Herbert Francis Murray RN, 1850 – 1870, *died at sea*
          - Harriet, *eldest sister of Francis Henry Murray*, d. 1854, *m. George Charles, 2nd Marquis Camden. Two of their daughters, Lady Augusta Pratt and Lady Eleanor Pratt, lived at St Nicholas' Rectory during the last years of the Rector's life*
        - Amelia, *fourth daughter*, 1795 – 1884, *Maid of Honour to Queen Victoria*
  - Lord Charles, *Jacobite*, 1691 - 1720
  - Lord George, *Jacobite general at Culloden*, 1694 – 1760, m. Amelia Murray
    - **John**, **3rd Duke of Atholl**, **1729 - 1774** (see above)

This pedigree shows only those members of the Murray family mentioned in the text

Chapter 1

Ancestry

Frederic, in this chapel are ancestors; you cannot deny that.
With the estate, I bought the chapel and its contents.
I don't know whose ancestors they were, but I know whose ancestors they are . . .

GILBERT AND SULLIVAN, *The Pirates of Penzance.*

Authenticated ancestors of note are indeed an asset in life and, in contrast to the parvenu Major-General Stanley in *The Pirates of Penzance*, Francis Henry Murray was well blessed with generation upon generation of worthy, and not-so-worthy, forebears. His own father, George Murray (1784-1860), was a Bishop, his grandfather was a Bishop and previous to him there was a line of three dukes who, in their turn, were preceded by earls and marquises. The family had always engaged in an ambitious mix of fighting and politics.

FHM's mother was born Lady Sarah Maria Hay-Drummond, daughter of the ninth Earl of Kinnoull: she is buried in Chislehurst and her grave is to be found near the west wall of the churchyard, on the north side. FHM was her second son in a family of six surviving daughters and five sons.

Sadly, as so often happens with mothers, not a lot is recorded of the life and achievements of Lady Sarah herself but a charming anecdote concerning a previous Lord Kinnoull goes thus: George Frederick Handel, on being complimented by Lord Kinnoull on the noble performance of the Messiah which he had lately given responded 'My Lord, I should be sorry if I only entertained them: I wish to make them better!'

FHM's grandfather, Lord George Murray (1761-1803), became Bishop of St David's in 1801 but his untimely death, less than three years after his consecration, denied him the chance to prove himself in that capacity: he had caught a chill waiting for his carriage on leaving the House of Lords. However, in the manner of many 18th and 19th century clergymen,[1] he had found the leisure to devote himself to alternative occupations and had made a name for himself in a decidedly useful enterprise before being created Bishop of St David's.

In the 1790s the country was in a flurry over the threat of Napoleonic invasion and news of the new French system of communication by signalling highlighted England's need to rival this development if she were to be alert to the invasion when it came. The French system was bettered by Lord George Murray in its simplicity. The French, using the 'T-telegraph' developed by Claude Chappe, could convey 9,999 separate words, all listed in a code book: the words were transmitted by what would look like, to modern eyes, a jaunty television aerial. The advantage of Lord George's invention was that it could convey words, letter by letter, and this was by means of six movable shutters on a 3 x 2 frame. (This can be compared to the arrangement of six dots used in Braille.) Six shutters, or selections from them, can be arranged in sixty-four different ways (one of them being unusable in this context) and so, with only twenty-six letters in the alphabet, there was scope also for the inclusion of useful phrases and the ten numerals. For reading the messages, only the code for each arrangement of shutters was required. However, there was no secret whatsoever about the codes: they were public knowledge for those who were interested.

The Shutter Mechanism. Drawn by John G. Stewart, 1984

Lord George Murray's 'shutter telegraph' was adopted for use across the South of England and, with a reward of £2,000, Lord George was granted the management of the telegraphs. His shutters were placed on the roofs of specially constructed cottages which were built at intervals on high ground between London and Portsmouth and Deal in Kent, one being situated at the top of Green Lane, Chislehurst. An average message could be relayed between London and Portsmouth in fifteen minutes and a pre-arranged signal relayed and acknowledged in just two minutes.

The drawback for both the French and English signalling systems was their dependence on clear weather (this was also true for the naval system of messaging by flags) and visual telegraphy was ousted eventually by the advent of electrically transmitted Morse Code in the 1850s.

So much for the busy life of the eighteenth century parson! In addition to his exciting work for the Admiralty Lord George Murray was at that time the Archdeacon of Sodor and Man, Rector of Hunton in Kent, and Dean of Bocking in Essex.

FHM was forever proud of the achievements of his grandfather and possessed a working model of the shutter which, he made clear in his will, he wished to remain in the family.

Above Lord George Murray in the family tree come the first three Dukes of Atholl. There are some important points to raise about them but their lives were of such great complexity that to talk about them in detail would be tedious. What follows is but a list that takes us to where we want to be in the narrative and it shows the extent to which the Murrays were involved in national events.

JOHN, THE 1st DUKE, (1660-1724) had been a supporter of the Glorious Revolution whereby, in. 1688-89, the Protestant William III and his wife Mary II came to the throne.

John's second son William, Marquis of Tullibardine, suffered attainder; that is, lost his right to inherit the title (his elder brother had been killed at the battle of Malplaquet in 1709) and the vast estates which were said to amount to two-thirds of the county of Perthshire. William's treasonable part in the Jacobite Rebellion of 1715 was the reason for the attainder and furthermore, he still maintained his Jacobite loyalty in the 1745 uprising. [see below]

John's third son, James, therefore succeeded to the Dukedom as the 2nd Duke of Atholl, this being clarified by an Act of Parliament which debarred William and his heirs from inheritance, for ever.

John's fifth son, George, (like William and the fourth son Charles) espoused the Jacobite cause and as lieutenant-general, George was, in effect, the Jacobite commander in the 1745 rebellion. He was a superb leader: he was responsible for victory at Prestonpans, Clifton and Falkirk and it is generally agreed that, had his fellow-Jacobite leaders heeded his warnings, fewer men would have died in the horrific massacre of Culloden.

The Atholl family at this time was seriously divided.

JAMES, THE 2nd DUKE, (1690-1764) inherited the sovereignty of the Isle of Man in 1737[2] but the family seat remained Blair Castle in Perthshire. During the 1745 uprising he fled south and lost, temporarily, the family seat at Blair to the attainted elder brother, William. Demonstrating his loyalty by marching northwards with the Duke of Cumberland ('Butcher Cumberland') he was able to regain his estates. Without surviving male issue the succession could have proved troublesome except that James's daughter Charlotte inherited, on her father's death in 1764, the sovereignty of the Isle of Man and, ten years before, had conveniently married her cousin, John, son of Lord George Murray, the Jacobite leader.

JOHN, THE 3rd DUKE, (1729-1774) was aware that Jacobite family connections could be a disadvantage and he therefore petitioned the king that his claim to the Dukedom might be allowed. It was, but not without constraints: in effect, the Duke and Duchess had to sell to the Treasury their sovereignty of the Isle of Man (for £70,000). But by payment of a yearly sum to the Crown they retained their landed property, the patronage of the Bishopric and the control of the fisheries, minerals etc. and, in addition, they received an annuity of £2,000 for the rest of their lives. So, all in all, they did quite well out of the arrangement except that from this point onwards they became intensely unpopular on the island and this unpopularity eventually forms part of Francis Henry Murray's story.

The Right Reverend Lord George Murray, he of the shutter mechanism, was the fourth son of the third Duke. Lord George's second son became another Bishop George Murray, father to FHM. In 1820, the year of FHM's birth, the family was living on the Isle of Man: the reference on the first page of FHM's recollections in Webb's *History of Chislehurst* hints at the reason for their hurried departure a few years later.

1 Gilbert White of Selborne, Edmund Cartwright and Thomas Malthus, to name but three.
2 Through his descent from the Earls of Derby on his mother's side.

Chapter 2

The Murray Family and the Isle of Man

. . . he was obliged to leave the island on account of the riots and great personal danger.

WEBB, MILLER and BECKWITH, *The History of Chislehurst.*

When the Isle of Man came under the sovereignty of the Second Duke of Atholl in 1737 it was already a thorn in the flesh of the government because the islanders displayed inconvenient signs of independence. On religious matters they claimed to be the only Protestant nation in Europe never to have been excommunicated: they had dispensed with the Papacy one hundred years before any other nation. Furthermore, they had an unusual degree of Home Rule in that they possessed what they claimed to be the oldest legislative assembly in the world, the House of Keys. And most inconvenient of all was the fact that the main industry of the island was smuggling, a profitable activity which was depriving the government of vast sums in customs revenue. The Isle of Man needed to be vested in the Crown before this problem could be even half resolved.

It was the threat to their smuggling activities which most infuriated the islanders when the Third Duke, the last to be styled 'Lord of Man', sold out to the government in 1765. They felt equally misused by the Atholls' retention of mineral rights for the island had become no more than a useful source of income for the Atholl family.

The Fourth Duke of Atholl (1755-1830) was appointed 'Governor' of the Isle of Man and in 1814, claiming his right to church patronage on the island, he appointed his nephew George to the Bishopric of Sodor and Man; George was thirty years of age. He had been made Archdeacon of Sodor and Man in 1806, aged twenty two, and had married Lady Sarah Hay-Drummond in 1811. In 1820 Francis Henry Murray, their second son, was born at the episcopal residence known as Bishop's Court.

The appointment brought the unpopularity of the Atholls to a head. At that time, nepotism was so common that it was generally unquestioned and so this in itself did not greatly infuriate the Manx people. However, George Murray, displaying a disastrous lack of judgement, made the great error of trying to add to his modest stipend of £1,000 a year. He aimed to achieve this by the revival of an old perk which had at one time been awarded to the Bishop: he claimed the right to a tithe of all the green and growing crops on the island. As a test case, the tithe on potatoes was brought to the judgement of the King in Council and the King pronounced in favour of the Bishop, thereby provoking riots which required the presence of troops from the mainland. At great speed and in some danger, the Bishop, his wife and young children (Francis being less than five years of age) retreated to live at Castle Mona, the Duke of Atholl's residence, before finally escaping the island in 1825.

With ruffled feathers they resorted to Bath, frequently a haven for those seeking mental or physical recuperation, and two years later the family moved to the Palace at Bromley on George's appointment to the Bishopric of Rochester.

Nothing can excuse George Murray's insensitive handling of the tithe but he was generally high-handed on many matters. He found the Church in a scandalous state on the island and felt compelled to rid himself of several priests. He was unpopular with most of the seventeen clergy of the See for he displayed 'a certain haughtiness of manner which wounded susceptibilities by a suggestion of social contempt'.[1] Their suspicions may well have been correct for when inviting the Rev. Benjamin Philpot to join him as a member of the island's clergy he commented, in the course of explaining his reasons, that there was not a 'gentleman with a white tie in the island'! The fact that he wanted the help of a 'gentleman' and 'scholar' arouses some sympathy: after all, he was a graduate of Christ Church, Oxford. No doubt he felt isolated, both culturally and academically, for according to Benjamin Philpot the island was in a primitive and poverty-stricken state: drinking amongst the poor was a pressing problem and the parochial system was in abeyance. *Insular* would truly be the word to describe both attitudes and geography, especially as the Manx tongue was still the language of the lower classes.

The traits of arrogance and avarice were to surface at intervals in George Murray's life. He was over-conscious of his noble background, he was typically High Tory and High Church and no description of him fails to mention the fact that he was the very last bishop to be seen in a clerical wig. He was firmly against any hint of the Roman Church in Anglican services but he had no truck with Dissenters either. When Durham University was founded he supported the idea that, as at Oxford and Cambridge, there should be no degrees awarded to Dissenters. He was not particularly isolated in this view.

His strong views on Dissenters were not to be modified. In 1860 the Prime Minister, Lord Palmerston, in a letter to Queen Victoria, commented: ' . . . the late Bishop of Carlisle and the late Bishop of Rochester, two kind-hearted and good-natured men, refused to consecrate burial grounds unless a wall of separation divided the portion allotted to Churchmen from the portion allotted to Dissenters – a demand which gave offence to both communities'.

Rather more outrageously, when bishops were asked whether they would accept Durham degrees to qualify men for Holy Orders there were just two bishops who declined: Rochester and Hereford 'disapproved of encouraging the lower classes to aspire to stations for which there were already too many candidates from the classes immediately above them'.[2]

An intriguing start to his Episcopacy at Rochester was the fact that he did not attend his own enthronement on 28th December, 1827 – but then, the Archbishop of Canterbury was not present either.[3] Each of them declined to attend and the ceremony was conducted by two teams of Proctors, six from Canterbury and six from Rochester.

It is only too easy to build an unfair picture of Murray around anecdotes but the view is somewhat rectified by a study of his Charge of 1843: this will be attempted in Chapter 4. He was to award livings in Kent to his three clerical sons: at Stone,

Southfleet and Chislehurst where, of course, FHM was incumbent for fifty six years. For these three clerics the Bishop's Charge was an instruction from both their father and their Bishop, their Father in God.

1 A.G. Bradley, *Our Centenarian Grandfather*. (A biography of Benjamin Philpot, Archdeacon of Sodor and Man until 1838.)

2 Owen Chadwick, *The Victorian Church*, Part 1.

3 Rochester Chapter Red Book.

The Bishop of Rochester

Chapter 3

Education

stet fortuna domus

Motto of Harrow School

By the time the family took up residence in the Bishop's Palace at Bromley, in 1827, it had grown into a considerable body of people requiring a substantial income. This was after sixteen years of marriage. However, the new Right Reverend Father in God, George by Divine Permission Lord Bishop of Rochester had, by this appointment, been downgraded to £1,500 per annum. The drop in income was partly rectified a few months later by his being nominated, in addition, Dean of Worcester. What seemed like a contrived arrangement did not, in fact, indicate yet more machinations by the Bishop: because of the poverty of the See of Rochester there had been a long understood agreement whereby the Bishop could hold another benefice *in commendam*.[1]

In 1836 Bishop Murray bargained with the Ecclesiastical Commission for the £4,500 per annum which, by the Established Church Act of 1836, any successor in Rochester would receive: if he could be paid at this level he would relinquish Worcester. The Established Church Act succeeded in banning the holding of benefices *in commendam* but somehow, Bishop Murray managed to cling on to Worcester for a further nine years until, in 1845, he handed over to Edward, brother of Robert Peel, the Prime Minister.

The parallel appointments to the Bishopric of Rochester and the Deanery of Worcester meant that the young FHM may have spent his childhood in the two places. However, it would not have been unusual if the Dean of Worcester had never visited the city but had remained in Bromley at the palace of the Bishop of Rochester. The Bishop's Palace, now in Civic use, was a residence of gracious and satisfying proportions.

One can only suppose that FHM was tutored at home until the age of twelve. However, we do know that he and his elder brother George Edward (b. 1818) started their three years at Harrow School in 1832.

* * *

Why Harrow should have been chosen is not clear. It was not in the same league as the three prototype 'public schools', Eton, Winchester and Westminster, for it had its roots in a charity school of 1324. It was then re-founded in 1571 on the basis of a charter drawn up by John Lyon, a local landowner. Nevertheless, by 1832, the fees were just as high as at any of the top schools and when FHM and his brother enrolled it was well on the way to becoming an exclusive boarding school for the sons of aristocrats. This development caused much fury in local residents who believed, quite rightly, that the original founder had endowed the school for local boys. The problem was that the endowments were not very extensive and there was also a strangling stipulation that the Governors must maintain certain roads. The inevitable happened: in order to make more money, pupils from elsewhere ('foreigners' as they were originally known) were brought into masters' houses resulting in increased tuition fees for the school as a whole and, more importantly, generous incomes to the masters. For the masters, especially those who set themselves up to run a 'house', Harrow was a lucrative attraction with advantages over academic positions at Oxford or Cambridge where remuneration was poor and marriage was forbidden. So, in the time of the young Murrays, all masters were ordained and many were of high academic calibre although usually so far removed in intellect from most of their charges that they were ineffective teachers. Many did as little teaching as possible. Harrow staff were well-known for their gold-digging and opportunism: bringing up the children of nobility forged contacts with influential families who could facilitate future promotion outside the world of education. In a letter of congratulation to a newly appointed member of staff in 1826 John Keble lightheartedly hoped that he would be remembered 'when you become a bishop in consequence of your judicious operations upon the head or heels or whatever it may be on any little Duke or Prime Minister'.[2]

Education is an idealistic word for what went on in these schools of the eighteenth and nineteenth centuries. Even the top three schools were notorious for wild behaviour and near-impossible conditions for academic progress. Edward Thring, later to be the enlightened Headmaster of Uppingham School, made the following observation about his time at Eton: 'Cruel at times the suffering and wrong; wild the profligacy. For after eight o'clock at night no prying eyes came near until the following morning; no-one lived in the same building; cries of joy and pain were equally unheard; and, excepting a code of laws of their own, there was no help or redress for anyone'.[3]

Defining the idea of what a school should be and do was undertaken by Thomas Arnold at Rugby (he went there as Headmaster in 1827) but, as yet, his innovations were being watched with suspicion and cynicism. He tried to harness the tradition of 'boy-rule', a feature of all these early schools, and make out of it a training in leadership and responsibility.

At Harrow, the mayhem of the 1820s under the headship of George Butler was not quelled by the next Headmaster, Charles Longley (1794-1868), who was elected in 1829 and covered the three years of FHM's time there. The outstanding failings of Butler's régime could be summed up as: endemic bullying; an erratic system of flogging by both staff and senior pupils; no secure lock-up system; little incentive for academic work and a poor curriculum. These problems were still not addressed in Longley's time and therefore give a clear background to FHM's experience of Harrow. Longley eventually progressed to be Archbishop of Canterbury and figured in the life of FHM at a later date. But his time at Harrow was summed up thus in the *Dictionary of National Biography*: 'Longley was elected headmaster of Harrow

School in 1829. He remained there for seven years, and although the number of boys grew under his rule from 115 to 165, much laxity of discipline prevailed'.

In a lively account of life at Harrow between 1829 and 1835 the 'laxity of discipline' is vividly described.[4] To be fair, each boarder did possess a small study with a surface for writing where a 'swot' would write his verses and learn his Homer but the unscrupulous would copy out the verses which they had induced others to write for them. Each study had its toasting fork for the preparation of breakfast and tea but this also served as a cruel instrument of torture for small boys who had slipped up on their fagging duties.

Food was unattractive and inadequate, tempting boys to run up exorbitant bills in local shops. Official flogging, organised by the Headmaster, was not considered a degradation but rather an opportunity to show unflinching courage. Fighting between the boys was connived at by the masters even when conflicting parties gathered in threatening groups on the traditional fighting ground. When not expending their energies in combat the boys used up every spare minute of freedom in glorious occupations such as bird-catching, poaching, shooting, beagling and horse-riding. To be uninterested in field sports marked a boy out as a bit of a dud. The cult of sport was well established as it served to keep the boys occupied: cricket, for example, could be in progress for as many as twenty two hours in the week – taking up a good deal more time than academic lessons. Sport was entirely organised by the pupils themselves. More than sixty years later, when FHM was congratulating the successful cricket team of the St Nicholas' Schools, he recalled the fact that at Harrow he had once taken all the wickets of the opposing team in one innings!

Lessons, if such they could be called, were tedious and ill-disciplined for they were presented in a dry and formal manner: in effect, these sessions provided but token tuition for any real teaching had to be paid for separately with private tutors.

The curriculum consisted of Latin and Greek and any other topic was in the category of an 'extra'. Those who taught the 'extras' were held in low esteem, not really part of the establishment, and what they taught was similarly derided. Mathematics was certainly not part of the curriculum,[5] nor was there any form of religious instruction. However, FHM and his brother did have one advantage: they were placed in Kennedy's, that is, the house of Benjamin Hall Kennedy of *Kennedy's Revised Latin Primer* which is still available today.[6] After Harrow, Kennedy became Head of Shrewsbury School and after that, Regius Professor of Greek at Cambridge. He was to gain the reputation of being England's foremost teacher of Latin. At Harrow, Kennedy's house was slightly set apart and when he went there in 1830 at the age of twenty-six he immediately effected an improvement in the tone and the academic standards of his own house. So it could be that FHM and his brother had a better experience of Harrow than most.

An obituary by Ernest J.A. Fitzroy authoritatively described FHM's loyalty to and love of Harrow. Fitzroy quoted from Mr Minchin's *Old Harrow Days*: 'Murray was at Harrow under Dr Longley in the house of Mr Kennedy, The Grove. It was strange to hear this saintly man [FHM] speak of having been flogged twice, and of his having had four thousand lines of Homer to write out in his Easter holidays. "I richly deserved this" he said "because I stoned a boy from a private school who was walking in The Grove." Then he added, "I should not have minded this had not my father met Dr Longley who told him." One of Murray's floggings was for letting off fireworks on Guy Fawkes' Day – the Protestant anniversary which one would not now connect with that eminent High Churchman. The discipline of the school seems to have been non-existent. Murray used to go out nightly, and was actually out skylarking in The Grove when Mr Kennedy sent for him to give him a learning prize. If this is the record of a good boy, what would be the record of a bad one?'

There was also a comment from FHM about one of the infamous Harrow masters, The Rev. Henry Drury, who had, incidentally, been Byron's tutor: 'He was completely past work . . . he used to eat fruit in class.' FHM apparently deplored the cold and formal services in the Parish Church where the masters sat apart in one pew, while the boys, isolated in the galleries, joined in neither the responses nor the singing.

Ernest Fitzroy continued with a description of FHM's enthusiasm for Old Boys' events. For example 'a few years ago he went up to Wigan to meet a few old schoolfellows at dinner and returned the next morning to preside at a meeting in Kent'.

This manifestation of the cult of Harrow was based on but three years' residence, for at the age of fifteen FHM left the school and he and his brother continued their preparation for Oxford under a tutor at home.[7] They both entered Christ Church in January of 1838.

* * *

FHM and his brother were respectively 17 and 19 years of age when they took up residence at Oxford, appearing in the matriculation list as *Franciscus Henricus Murray* and *Georgius Edwardus Murray*. That they should be sent to Oxford is no surprise: Bishop Murray was himself an alumnus of Christ Church and, indeed, all five of his sons were up at Christ Church. Later, FHM's elder son was also to go. More importantly, Oxford University was the powerhouse of the Established Church. Geoffrey Faber sums up the Oxford of the time, before the first Royal Commission in 1850: 'Men went to Oxford to receive the conventional education considered appropriate for a gentleman, whether they went afterwards into Parliament or resided upon their estates or took Holy Orders or were called to the Bar. The twin shadows of an Established Church and a self-satisfied order of society still lay thickly over the entire University. No young man was admitted unless he formally subscribed to the Thirty-Nine Articles of the Church of England. Once matriculated he must attend the services of his College chapel and receive Holy Communion once a term. In Oriel certainly (and no doubt in other colleges) he must attend the University Sermon on Sunday mornings and satisfy the authorities by a *précis* of its argument that he had listened to it with attention. He was governed and taught exclusively by clergymen. Any intellectual adventure outside the so-called Humanities and the walled city of

Classical Mathematics was at once difficult and dangerous. Even Theology was a post-graduate study, for it could not be safely approached until the rash speculations of youth had dissipated themselves into the void'.[8]

Geoffrey Faber continues: 'Oxford was close to being an all-male society. College Fellows were required to relinquish their Fellowship on marriage and many a man, waiting to marry but without the means to do so, lingered on as a College tutor, year after year, eating his heart out and weary of his office, until a College living came his way'.

Although Oxford was a serious place for some undergraduates it resembled the public schools of the day with its 'rabble' element. According to Frederick Oakeley: 'The undergraduate society of Christ Church . . . was split up into some half-dozen or more sets. There was an aristocratic set, a reading set, a hunting set, a boating set and some others too indefinite in their character to receive a distinctive appellation . . . The moral and religious tone . . . was anything but satisfactory. Late supper parties extensively prevailed, and frequently led to breaches of discipline which were visited with rustication or expulsion. The behaviour in Chapel was generally irreverent and sometimes disgraceful. Irregularity in attendance at Chapel was punished at Christ Church by impositions which usually consisted of one hundred lines of Virgil to be transcribed by a certain day; but this exercise was usually performed by a deputy.'[9]

The wilder element of the schools came up to Oxford and emerged as the expensive idlers, the sots and topers, who had no academic intentions whatsoever. For example, there exists a hand-written academic record of the termly achievements of the Christ Church undergraduates of FHM's time: three others share his page and each one went down from Oxford without completing the course – the Duke of Roxburghe (sic) survived but one term.

The record of 'Murray Jr' shows that he followed a standard Classics degree, including Mathematics, and there is evidence of some Theology. The comments on his termly oral examinations range from 'middling' to 'satisfactory' to 'very satisfactory' to '*optime*' all of which culminated in a Class III degree. An added distinction was that he was elected a Student (Christ Church terminology for Fellow) in 1839, which status he retained until his marriage in 1846, the year of his appointment to Chislehurst. Not too much should be read into the class of degree at that time for the system did not have the sophistication to label people with accuracy. Class IV no longer exists at Oxford but was well-populated in the 1840s.

At the end of his Oxford career in 1841 FHM took on the role of tutor to the Marquis of Chandos, later to be Duke of Buckingham, spending term time at Christ Church with him, and the vacation at Stowe or Wotton with the family.

In 1843 FHM was ordained Deacon by Bishop Bagot of Oxford. He served one year as a curate in Kidderminster and then two years as a curate in Northfield, now in Birmingham. It was in 1846 that he arrived in Chislehurst, still a country village with only three hundred and eighty houses and fewer than two thousand inhabitants. The church and Rectory were neglected buildings, there having been an absentee Rector, Rev. Francis Dawson, for some years.

This state of affairs, far from being a problem for the new incumbent, provided an ideal starting point for the execution of the new ideas absorbed at Oxford University. His time at Oxford coincided with the dramatic years of the Oxford Movement and Francis Henry Murray brought the revolution into Chislehurst.

donorum dei dispensatio fidelis

Motto of Harrow School

---

1 A benefice whose revenues were granted to a bishop in addition to his Diocesan emoluments. At one time, benefices could be held *in commendam* by laymen as well as clergy.

2 Quoted in Christopher Tyerman, *A History of Harrow School.*

3 Quoted in Vivian Ogilvie, *The English Public School.*

4 By William Oxenden Hammond Esq. of St Alban's Court, Kent: printed in *The Harrovian* in 1950.

5 It is amusing to note that FHM kept the tellers' note of the result of the local referendum, in 1890, on the topic of gaslighting for Chislehurst. It is in FHM's handwriting and has his signature but there is an unmistakable error in the addition.

6 In the interests of accuracy it must be pointed out that although Kennedy compiled the original Latin Primer the little-known truth is that his two daughters did the revision and raised it to the status of a classic.

7 In his memoirs in *The History of Chislehurst*, FHM made references to his viewing, in the company of his tutor, of the new railway near Greenwich and of his first journey by rail in 1837 but he does not mention the fact that he attended the Coronation of Queen Victoria. This honour was by virtue of his aunt's position as a Maid of Honour to the young Queen. Amelia Matilda Murray (1795-1884), fourth daughter of Lord George Murray, deserves a book of her own: she was an attractive personality; she travelled widely and published accounts of her journeys; she was a vigorous advocate for the abolition of slavery; she concerned herself with the plight of destitute and delinquent children; she published her ideas on education and wrote a volume of recollections. She did not marry: a truly modern woman but rather eccentric for the time.

8 Geoffrey Faber, *Oxford Apostles – a character study of the Oxford Movement.*

9 The Very Reverend Canon Oakeley, *Personal Recollections of Oxford from 1820 to 1845.*

Chapter 4

The Oxford Movement

The following Sunday, July 14th, Mr Keble preached the Assize Sermon in the University pulpit . . . I have ever considered, and kept the day, as the start of the religious movement of 1833.

JOHN HENRY NEWMAN: *Apologia pro Vita Sua.*

To make sense of the Oxford Movement of the nineteenth century it is necessary to go back to the Reformation of the sixteenth century: that is, to the first set of Ten Articles of faith drawn up at the request of Henry VIII in 1536 and to the First Prayer Book of Edward VI compiled in 1548 by a conference of scholars convened under the leadership of Archbishop Cranmer. The conference sought to bring together the existing rites as practised before the break with Rome, to cut out the Latin tongue from public and private worship, and by many adjustments to make intelligent worship accessible for *all* people. The Articles of Faith contained important doctrinal changes, especially in Eucharistic theology. The Act of Uniformity (January 1549) ordered the Prayer Book to come into general use.

After 1549 there were further editions of the Book of Common Prayer in 1552, 1559 and 1604. The 1662 edition appeared as a consequence of the Restoration of the Monarchy. This last edition is still authorised for use.[1]

The Act of Uniformity spoke of 'The Archbishop of Canterbury . . . and other learned men of this realm' as having been appointed by the King (Edward VI) to 'draw and make one convenient and meet order of rite and fashion of common and open prayer and administration of the sacraments, to be had and used in His Majesty's realm of England and Wales'. The Book of Common Prayer defined the liturgy and Articles of Religion for the 'Protestant' Church in England. However, whether or not the Church of England was, or is, 'Protestant' is arguable. At the Reformation, Protestantism sought to proclaim the inner being of the Church in terms of the Word of God rather than in sacramental relationships.

However, statutes cannot necessarily change men's hearts and minds nor smoothly eradicate habit, and in places the style of Roman Catholic devotion continued well into the reign of Elizabeth I. Indeed, English Catholics managed to survive, under cover and later openly, until their official emancipation was granted in 1829. Queen Elizabeth was herself an embarrassment to the Reformers as she retained the cross and lighted candles in her private chapel. At the same time there were many who had absorbed the Calvinistic model of reform and who could hardly wait to see the abolition of every relic of the Roman Church. The suppression of Roman Catholicism in the ensuing centuries is well known: the barbaric example made of the Gunpowder Plot confederates, the string of inhibiting Acts of Parliament and then the general loosening up of official attitudes which culminated in the Catholic Emancipation Act of 1829.

Popular feeling against Roman Catholics did not keep pace with legislation: there remained a latent suspicion of Roman Catholicism as being non-English. It signified allegiance to the Pope and allegiance to enemy Roman Catholic countries. The handy slogan 'No Popery' is still in use![2] Anti-Catholicism has a permanent place in the national psyche but with a growing choice of hate targets in modern society it is not the issue that it was, except for a more complicated version in Northern Ireland.

The instigators and heirs of the nineteenth century Oxford Movement sought to demonstrate that the Reformation 'settlement' was not satisfactory to all. They set out to prove that the link with the pre-Reformation Catholic Church had never been broken and that there was evidence in the Book of Common Prayer and Articles of Religion that provision had been made for the continuance of Catholic belief and devotion – without the necessity of allegiance to a Pope. This was not entirely novel for the High Church tradition had never been absent from the Church of England, and the Apostolic Succession, a *sine qua non* for a claim to Catholicity, had been finally settled by Archbishop Laud in the seventeenth century.[3]

The Book of Common Prayer had been designed as an aid to the imposition of uniformity, a bridge to hold together those of opposing tastes and beliefs. Such was the status of the Prayer Book that critics of the Oxford Movement could say that it seemed to be accorded equal authority with the Holy Scriptures. It is therefore not surprising that the Oxford Movement's extraction of Catholic outlook from what had always been considered a Protestant document should invoke charges of Romanism.

* * *

Why the Oxford Movement should have a supposed starting date of 1833 is no simple matter. It was only with hindsight that participators and onlookers could parcel the Oxford Movement into the next twelve years. The year 1845, with the defection of the charismatic John Henry Newman, was by no means the end of the matter.

Dissatisfaction with the Church of England was being articulated by a few members of Oxford Colleges, notably Oriel, in the years preceding 1833. Causes for discontent were the heavy dependence on the state; the worldliness, indeed the laziness, of too many bishops and clergy; the neglect of spirituality and devotion and, at a local level, the observation that the church was only too clearly dying.

Stories abound of the state of ordinary village churches in the first half of the nineteenth century[4] and the following is taken from the *Memories of Dean Hole*,[5] himself a follower of the Oxford Movement but who in fact never quite shook off his own 'hunting parson' image. He describes the village church of his youth: 'Our curate, who lived five miles away, rode over for one dreary service on the Sunday, dined, and we saw him no more during the week. He was much occupied in the pursuit of the fox, which, it is charitable to suppose, he mistook for a wolf and like a good shepherd was anxious to destroy. The service was literally a duet between the parson and the clerk, except when old John Manners, the bricklayer, gave the keynote for the hymn from his bassoon, a sound which might have been uttered by an elephant in distress, and we sang – "O turn my pi – O turn my pi – O turn my pious soul to Thee." Or when the curate suddenly emerged from his surplice, which he placed on the side of the reading pew, and appearing in his academical gown, went up the three-decker to preach. The altar was represented by a small rickety deal table, with a scanty covering of faded and patched green baize, on which were placed the overcoat, hat and riding whip of the officiating minister, who made a vestry within the sacrarium, and, sitting there in a huge surplice, had a conversation with the sexton before the service began, and looked as though he were about to have his hair cut. The font was filled with coffin ropes, tinder box and brimstone matches, candle ends etc. It was never used for baptism. The squire and his wife would never have countenanced such an unseemly interruption of the service. Sparrows twittered and bats floated beneath the rotten timbers of the roof, while beetles and moths and all manner of flies found happy homes below. The damp walls represented in fresco "a green and yellow melancholy" which had a depressing influence upon the spirit and the darkest and most dismal building of the parish was that called the House of God.'

Dean Hole's description hints at the main problems of the church at a local level. The fact that it was a curate who came over, not the incumbent, was significant: he would most likely have drawn stipends from one, two or even more livings and would have chosen to be resident at the one that best suited him. The curate would have dined with the Squire, thus putting the church and the main local employer at the same dinner table, and if employees had been at the church service it would have been because they were bound to be there if they valued their jobs or tied cottages. Sometimes a clergyman became a local magistrate and parishioners were therefore judged rather than comforted by their father in God.

The quoted passage reveals the tedium and the passive nature of the worship: the dilapidated state of the building speaks of the lack of leadership and enthusiasm in the village and the casual conduct of the service by the curate can hardly have been inspiring. Further on in his memories Dean Hole adds: 'There was not then the anxious forethought, the preliminary training, which are now bestowed upon those who are candidates for the priesthood. Too many young men were attracted by the leisure which seemed to accompany the life of a clergyman, and to a profession which brought ready admission into what is called good society. Some were to have rich livings by purchase, and some through family ties.'[6]

The slackness of the clergy had not been addressed because Convocation, the Church's 'Parliament' consisting of an Upper House of Bishops and a Lower House of Clergy, had been prorogued by royal writ since 1717. There was therefore no way of discussing and managing the Church at local or national level nor of developing a vision. This was the supreme contribution of the Oxford Movement – the vision of a renewed Church and clergy.

* * *

One of the inhibiting influences on the Church over the previous one hundred and fifty years had been, in an unsuspected way, the fact that it was the 'Established' Church. Protected by that legislation which had discriminated against Catholics and

Dissenters, the Clergy could sit back comfortably without having to proclaim anything.[7] However, protection was now being systematically dismantled by alarming liberal developments pushed through under Whig influence, not least the Reform Bill of 1832. Traditional Tory clergy feared for a future where the Church 'would find itself yoked with a partner whose ends and purposes might cover much that to a sound churchman would be repugnant'.[8] This fear was realised only too soon when the Whig Government, anxious to solve problems in Ireland where the electorate had nearly doubled as a result of the Reform Act, introduced the Church Temporalities (Ireland) Bill in February 1833. By this Bill ten out of the twenty two Bishoprics of the Church of Ireland were to be abolished and the income saved was to be distributed according to government decision.[9] There were many who saw the practical wisdom of this move but many others saw it as a secular, even profane, interference in Church affairs. At the same time the government's sympathy for Dissenters and Roman Catholics seemed to be marginalising the Established Church. These factors were the prompts for John Keble's[10] Assize Sermon in Oxford (see opening quotation) which he entitled 'National Apostasy' – apostasy being defined as the abandonment or renunciation of a religious belief or principle. Keble alerted churchmen to the Church's peril from increasingly secular and liberal attitudes in political life.

A more subtle threat was that of the growing liberalism in religious teaching: the Church, having slept through the eighteenth century, had not responded to the exploration of Biblical doubts nor did it heed the spread of Dissenting opinions in society as a whole. Evangelical fervour, 'enthusiasm', was there in abundance but what use was fervour and emotional individualism without doctrine? The time had come for a re-appraisal of the position of the Church of England and of the derivation of its authority. 'The liberal menace could be met only by recourse to the historic teachings of Catholic Christianity which the Church of England, despite the Reformation, had preserved in its formularies and which the best of its divines had never sought to minimise. Hence, the Oxford School of the 1830s were far from claiming to be innovators. Their business was not to invent anything but to recall men to ancient truths that had far too long been overlooked or had ceased to stir the pulses of faith. To preach these truths therefore became a mission. An urgent work was to be done, the doing of which demanded not only learning and fixity of principle . . . but personal dedication and commitment which alone would arouse merely nominal Christians from spiritual lethargy and arm them to resist the forces under which all religious belief might in the end crumble.'[11]

So this was to be the work of the Oxford men who banded together to make their case. Their driving motive was to encourage increased personal holiness and they believed that this was possible through membership of the Church, provided that the Church herself was in proper order. The Church needed to be reminded of her ancient authority and her heritage of spiritual riches.

The leading spirit of the group was John Henry Newman, Fellow of Oriel College, Oxford, since 1822, and Vicar of the University Church of St Mary the Virgin from 1828. To encapsulate in a few paragraphs Newman's contribution to the proceedings

John Henry Newman

of the Oxford Movement is to risk diminishing him: happily, for those who are interested, there is a vast bibliography of texts relating to his life, including his own *Apologia pro Vita Sua* (1864), a history of his religious opinions. He happened to be abroad when the Assize Sermon was preached but he and others had nevertheless been passionately disturbed already about the state of the Church and desired to take some kind of action. He returned to England with a decision to take a leaf out of the evangelicals' book and use a pamphlet campaign: indeed, until Oxford, Newman had been within the evangelical fold. A series of topical pamphlets, *Tracts for the Times,* appeared over the next eight years composed by himself and friends such as John Keble, Hurrell Froude, Isaac Williams, Edward Pusey[12] and others. The description 'Tractarians' first appeared in print in 1838.

Initially, the writers claimed to be setting up a case against Popery and Dissent but they thereby covered a wide range of topics. The stated aim of the Tracts was 'to arrest the advance of Liberalism in religious thought' and to revive what the writers held to be 'the true conception of the relation of the Church of England to the Catholic Church at large.'[13] However reactionary these aims appear to be there is an opinion that the movement was part of the 'general cultural renaissance denoted by the word romanticism'.[14] There was more to it than Politics and Religion. 'Religion as they [the pioneers of the Oxford Movement] saw it was not simply a matter of doctrines and rites, but of the life of prayer and worship, the sense of eternity, the discipline of the self's wayward desires . . . a spiritual awakening of spiritual wants.'[15]

The early Tracts were only brief pamphlets: four pages was the recommended length. Later ones would better be described as extended scholarly treatises. They were read by churchmen and lay people alike but those who responded most energetically were, on the whole, bishops and clergy. Many of these found they were already tuned in, albeit subconsciously, to the truths being championed and rallied enthusiastically to the cause. Many others could only see the slippery slope to Rome. The vocabulary and titles alone could make this latter group shiver: Eucharist, fasting, devotions, Apostolic Succession and celibacy were common enough words but enabled antagonists to sniff out Popery. '*Reserve in Communicating Religious Knowledge*' (Tract LXXX by Isaac Williams) was an example of a controversial title. To those who took on the mind of the Oxford Movement it was 'a protest against the coarseness and shallowness which threw the most sacred words about at random'.[16] In other words, a protest against evangelical ways. To those who were *not* of the mind of the Oxford Movement it sounded like a devious withholding of the full truth – an approach tainted with Jesuitry.

What Newman sought was the middle way, *Via Media* (Tract XXXVIII): 'The glory of the English Church is that it has taken the *Via Media* . . . it lies between the (so-called) Reformers and the Romanists'. Nevertheless, for a variety of reasons, the Tractarians attracted adherents of a Romeward tendency and this was to be a handicap: in a campaign which aimed at the renewal of the Church of *England* it was confusing to have this tension.

Tract XC in 1841, by Newman, brought controversy to a head and the contents were such that the Heads of Houses at Oxford protested loudly, questions were asked in Parliament and the Bishop of Oxford ordered the cessation of the Tracts. This last Tract was entitled *Remarks on Certain Passages in the Thirty-Nine Articles*. A key passage in the introduction reads: ' . . . while our Prayer Book is acknowledged on all hands to be of Catholic origin, our Articles also, the offspring of an un-Catholic age, are, through God's good providence, to say the least, not un-Catholic, and may be subscribed to by those who aim at being Catholic in heart and doctrine'.

Ever since the Movement had got off the ground Newman had seen that it would be necessary to appeal to early authorities of the primitive Church: this was his technique in Tract XC. Furthermore, since 1838 there had appeared volumes of *The Library of the Fathers*, English translations of selected writings of the Early Christian Fathers. Without going into the crafted conclusions of Tract XC it is clear that he was pushing the Catholicity point too far to be tolerated and this was now the end of the Movement – or so it seemed.

Newman, still convinced of the reality and credibility of the Church of England, went into partial seclusion at Littlemore, a village near Oxford. Peace was not possible there – partly because news got about that Littlemore was but a newly formed monastery where candidates for Rome were to be nurtured. Curious visitors were therefore constantly arriving and this was a source of extreme annoyance to Newman: for him, the news of each secession to Rome was truly a source of deep anguish. For men to desert the Church of England was never his intention: 'I desired a union with Rome under conditions, *Church with Church*'.[17]

The Bishops in their respective Charges to their Dioceses denounced the Oxford men. The Bishop of Rochester, for example, emphatically warned his clergy against 'adopting those novel views of your duty which are now insisted upon by the self-appointed and unauthorised reformers of our Church'.

Newman's state of mind during these years is shown by fragments from his *Apologia pro Vita Sua*. 'From the end of 1841 I was on my deathbed as regards my membership with the Anglican Church.' He likened himself to a sick and dying man in a tedious decline, not allowed to die in peace. About the ill-feeling of his friends he wrote: '. . . few could help me, few could understand me, many were annoyed with me, some were angry because I was breaking up a compact party and some, as a matter of conscience, would not listen to me'. About his doubts on the nature of the Church of England and the results of his long agony of allegiance he finally wrote: 'When I was fully confident that the Church of Rome was the only true Church, I joined her'. That was in 1845.

* * *

What a bizarre turn of events! What sorrow to the protagonists! What joy to the antagonists! However, by the time the final decision was made it did not come as a surprise to those who knew him and had pleaded with him. His resignation in 1843 from the living of St Mary the Virgin was a significant moment in the refining of his conscience, for his fifteen years there had allowed him more influence over Oxford than any number of Tracts. He transformed what had hitherto been simply a parish church situated in, admittedly, a prime position in the High Street into what was deemed to be the 'University Church'. According to Geoffrey Faber: 'His pupils at Oriel naturally followed him on to the sacred ground. He could not help writing his sermons with them in mind. His reputation as a preacher grew with astonishing swiftness. Other undergraduates from other colleges caught the contagion from Oriel. Young dons followed suit. In a short space of time the Sunday afternoon parish service and sermon at St Mary's became a *de facto* University institution far better attended and more influential than the two University Sermons. The English public at large, even many of the country clergy, got it into their heads that Newman preached in the "University Church" by University appointment.'[18]

Not only was the content of his sermons compelling, but the poetry of his language had an extraordinary effect as did also his ability to vary the pace and volume of his words: young men flocked to hear him. 'The service was very simple – no pomp, no ritualism[19] . . . the most remarkable thing was the beauty, the silver intonation, of Mr Newman's voice, as he read the lessons. It seemed to bring new meaning out of the original words . . .'[20]

He preached 604 sermons at St Mary's and thousands of students would have experienced the phenomenon in those fifteen years. The Cambridge History of English Literature said of Newman's sermons: 'There had been nothing like them in the English pulpit'. Francis Murray *must* have been one of those students. He was at Oxford as an undergraduate from 1838 until 1841 and then remained in Oxford when tutoring the Marquis of Chandos until ordained Deacon in 1843. There is no evidence available, other than the ambitions and achievements of his life, to be able to state that he was caught up in the Oxford Movement during his time at Oxford but that he was an observer and follower there is no doubt.

His father, the Bishop, did not want the clergy of his diocese (into which FHM was instituted in 1846) to show any Romish tendencies but he was in favour of the cultivation of personal holiness, the greater importance of orderly church services and the improvement of church buildings. His Charge of 1843 was a wise and careful document revealing a very different George Murray of Rochester from the George Murray of Sodor and Man.

It is interesting to think of FHM taking up his post in Chislehurst in 1846: what was his vision for Chislehurst? Did the Oxford Movement bear fruit through his life and work? Although all had seemed lost at the defection of Newman in 1845 the disaster only served to imbue the remaining members, together with a new wave of enthusiasts, with greater determination. The Movement did not die but thrived on the continuing opposition.

The Rev. S.L. Ollard, a historian of the Oxford Movement, listed its achievements in a pamphlet entitled *'What England owes to the Oxford Movement'* (1923).

> 'It changed the conception of worship throughout the Church of England, and by repercussion, the standard of worship in many Nonconformist bodies as well.'
> 'It inspired not only a desire to build churches, it inspired artists capable of building them.'
> 'It produced great hymn-writers, it inspired a new zeal for church music and it altered the place of music in worship.'
> 'Its leaders were not only religious men, they were scholars and it was inevitable that in literature they should leave their mark.' Newman, Keble, Pusey, Faber, Christina Rossetti, J.M. Neale etc.[21]
> 'It brought religion to bear on social questions, both in thought and in action.'
> 'One good result of the Revival was the restoration of the Community life in the Church of England.'

The following chapters will reveal how faithfully FHM played his part in the work and growth of the Oxford Movement.

---

1 An attempted twentieth century revision was passed by the Convocations and the Church Assembly but was controversially rejected by the House of Commons in 1927.

2 An example is the appearance of 'No Popery' banners carried on the fringes of the Anglo-Catholic processions in Walsingham, Norfolk.

3 Laud (1573-1645) sought to restore something of the pre-Reformation liturgical practice of the Church and he maintained that the Roman Catholic Church and the Church of England are both parts of the same Church Catholic. He was executed in 1645 after repudiating the accusation of Popery and declaring his adherence to the Protestant Church of England. (*Oxford Dictionary of the Christian Church.*)

4 Unfortunately there is no detailed description of St Nicholas', Chislehurst, at this time but the fact that the previous Rector to FHM was more or less absent for nine years indicates that some of the common criticisms may well have been applicable. There would have been a curate in attendance.

5 Sometime Dean of Rochester.
6 Dean Hole's *Memories* were first published in 1892.
7 Compare with the Methodists whose energy and commitment won thousands who had never set foot in a church.
8 Bernard M.G. Reardon, *Religious Thought in the Victorian Age.*
9 In 1869 the Church of Ireland was disestablished and separated from the Church of England.
10 John Keble (1792-1866). For a full biography of John Keble see the life by G. Battiscombe (1963).
11 Bernard M.G. Reardon, *op. cit.*
12 Edward Bouverie Pusey (1800-1882). This period of Pusey's life is covered in D. Forester's *Young Doctor Pusey* (1989).
13 The Churchman's Guide.
14 Bernard M.G. Reardon, *op. cit.*
15 Bernard M.G. Reardon, *op. cit.*
16 R.W. Church, *The Oxford Movement, Twelve Years: 1833-1845.*
17 J.H. Newman, *Apologia pro Vita Sua.*
18 Geoffrey Faber, *Oxford Apostles.*
19 The original men of the Oxford Movement had little patience with ritualism deeming it less important than the message they were putting across.
20 Quoted by Geoffrey Faber, *op. cit.*
21 Some more modern examples of Anglo-Catholic writers who have written, often with great humour, are Rose Macaulay, Dorothy L. Sayers, Barbara Pym and P.D. James. Also T.S. Eliot and A.N. Wilson.

Chapter 5

The First Four Years in Chislehurst

Two more united hearts than theirs
Were never found beneath the stars,
Through life or e'en to death.

ANNE ANDERDON, *A History of the Anderdon Family.*

In the absence of FHM's personal correspondence, a long poem by Anne Anderdon about the Manning and Anderdon families provides the closest possible approach to Francis Henry Murray himself.

Anne Anderdon and her sister Maria are known in Chislehurst for their founding of St Michael's Orphanage (1855) and also the Manning and Anderdon Almshouses (1881). Anne Anderdon's poem is a remarkable document: it consists of at least two thousand lines, hand-written in a small gold-embossed leather booklet. It was probably composed over many years. Its original purpose was to remind John, her younger brother destined to become head of the family, of his proud lineage and of the chief events in the family's history. However, towards the end of the poem, she records John's death in 1872. She herself died in 1892 and she is buried in St Nicholas' churchyard on the north side, close to her parents, John Lavicount Anderdon and Anna Maria.

With the help of this work and the collection of Anderdon family letters it is possible to experience something of their loving family life and gain some additional knowledge of events in Chislehurst.

The following extract gives Anne's picture of St Nicholas' Church before FHM's first alterations: she is describing what the new incumbent found when he came in 1846.

And soon the Rector's care was bent
that churchyard to improve.
He banished thence the cropping sheep
and left the graves in quiet sleep
which now we love so dear.

And the attention due he gave
to check the inner shrine
which had with high pews encumber'd been
and though there was a chancel screen
of old oak carved and fine,
nought else of any note was there.

At West end hung a gallery
where, seated in supreme command,
a poorly tuned-up village band
sent a discordant cry.

And through the church's central space
stained wood and green baize vie;
or high pews ranged from door to door
and children played about the floor
unseen by Master's eye.

In such a state the poor old church
two centuries had lain
and some brave courage was required
to make the improvements, much desired,
nor give the Ancients pain:
for 'tis the natural tendency
of ev'ry human mind
to love the things our fathers loved
and think that what they well approved
is best for us designed.

Two 'ungraceful' galleries in the chancel were removed and the walls scraped clean. 'Seats of oak' were fixed between the screen and the altar. As soon as this area

by permission of the PCC

The Church before the arrival of Francis Murray

had been smartened up the effect was such that all agreed that the remaining portion must have equal attention.

And this, with heart and will at work
they with each other vied;
parishioners and friends compete
the church's beauty to complete.

Anne gives the impression that, united, the people of Chislehurst converged on the church, shirtsleeves rolled up, ready to continue the half-finished job. She glosses over the fact that much committee work, money-raising and the Bishop's permission were necessary before further work could be attempted.

The new Rector was not solely concerned with the appearance of the church but also with the fresh appeal of the worship there. Anne Anderdon even goes so far as to attribute Chislehurst's spate of new housing to the attractiveness of the church.

The worship was his chiefest care
and earnestness in praise and prayer
his inmost soul's intent.
Thus cared for, Chislehurst became
a centre of attraction new.
For earnestness aye wins men's hearts
and many came from divers parts
and built their houses, not a few,
and so it is unto this day.

What FHM found at the Rectory was described in his hand-written notebook entitled *Things which my Successor should know about the House*. Here he outlined the alterations and additions to the house during his years in Chislehurst. 'When I came here in May 1846 the whole garden had been destroyed – my predecessor[1] was not resident for the nine years previous to 1846. He let the garden ground to a person here, Mr Bright.' Mr Bright had put the garden down to turnips, potatoes and mangel. FHM applied for damages and eventually received £20 having paid out £15 in costs.

The house was in a '*very* bad condition' and FHM received compensation for dilapidation. The whole of the west side of the house had to be taken down and new building took place. The Dining Room was singled out as being particularly dull, 'the panelling all painted stone colour with windows opening only to the north'.

FHM was to continue making improvements to the Rectory and gardens for the rest of his life. In his will he states: 'I have, during my incumbency, built a house on part of the Glebe known by the name of THE CLERGY HOUSE and I have also built three cottages thereon. If, at my death, I am possessed of any interest therein I bequeath the same to my successor in the Rectory for his use as Rector.'[2]

* * *

Back now to Anne Anderdon's poem; she is the only source for the charming courtship and marriage of FHM to Fanny, her young sister. Francis and Fanny were married in 1846. The Anderdons were, at that time, living in Reigate. (For more about this family see Chapter 8: they eventually settled in Chislehurst and remained closely bound up with the Rector's household.) The Anderdon family consisted of John, and Anna Maria (of the Manning family) with their children William, Maria[3] (known as 'Yi'), Anne, Fanny, John and 'little Helen'.

In her poem Anne describes how happy they were in Reigate: William was the new curate of the church of St Laurence and 'we sisters employment found in helping William in his parish round'. John, to whom the poem was addressed, had always been

by permission of Cdr Nigel Anderdon

Francis Murray as a young man

the special favourite of Fanny and

> every leisure time he'd aye engage
> her for some cozy talk or turn the page
> together of some quaint amusing book

but alas, inevitably, he went away to Eton and then on to Oxford. To Anne, all change was lamentable and even Eton and Oxford were cause for sorrow. Helen, however, was still at the stage of playing with 'young friends next door'.

Allowing for a sister's enthusiasm the description of Fanny is that of a specially talented young lady: brimful of fun, witty, good-tempered and graceful. She had a lovely voice and played with skill on the piano and the guitar. With her beauty and accomplishments she must have been the model of an early Victorian young lady.

Fanny had been invited by an aunt in town to spend the summer there: the family at home could not entirely understand why Fanny should want to spend so long away when she could have been at home in what was more or less the countryside. In spite of, or because of, the jolly time Fanny was enjoying, surrounded by much love and flattery, she and her aunt daily attended an eight o'clock church service. It was now that

> young Francis Murray came
> within their social circle – there to claim
> a nearer acquaintance with our sister dear.

They were a fairy tale pair, she being so very special and attractive and he being so handsome and 'excellently good'. All the same, it was noted by Anne that he was 'of a noble house' and that Fanny felt that she was not really good enough for him.

> So, when his suit was known and well approved,
> parents on both sides blessed the child they loved

and indeed, the wedding took place in the Autumn of the same year.

The wedding in Reigate 'truly was a bonny sight'. Friends and relatives gathered at the Anderdon house, by no means a large place, filling the drawing room and hall. So close was the church to the house that you could describe it as 'just at the garden gate' and therefore, instead of the customary carriages, the neighbourhood was treated to the sight of a procession on foot led by the Bishop of Rochester. He was followed by Fanny on the arm of her father who, though both happy and proud, was thinking also of the loss to the family circle that this would mean. Next came six bridesmaids followed by the bridegroom with his best man, one of his brothers. Two more of his brothers, both clergymen, were present as were the two remaining unmarried sisters.

After the service the procession and congregation made its way back to the house

> and found the festal board prepared
> as custom doth enforce.

And, at last, 'when the prancing steeds arrived before the door' the happy couple were driven away with the customary good wishes of all the guests. They went away to Canterbury, staying near the Cathedral, in rooms which belonged to a friend of the groom. After a month letters arrived and the parish began to intrude. They returned to Chislehurst where they set about their duties in the village and started to make the Rectory, as best they could, into a home. According to Anne's poem they succeeded well in both endeavours:

> Their home has aye a model been,
> where she was happy as a queen
> and he as any king.
> By turn, invited oft we went
> and aye it was our sweetest joy
> to see their bliss without alloy
> . . . and all the parish wisely ruled.

* * *

Over the next two years or so FHM was overseeing the changes to the church, changes needed on the grounds of an expanding population and changes needed to facilitate the improved style of worship that he had in mind. The chancel would have been, as always, the responsibility of the incumbent and FHM and friends had put up the necessary £500, but funds were needed for urgent re-pewing and a completely new aisle on the south side. Money was raised in two ways: Church Rate for the re-seating and a Subscription List for the new south aisle where at least two thirds of the space should be free and unappropriated. Orderly regimented pews would make for increased seating,[4] proper accommodation for kneeling and for a more attentive congregation but the achievement of the change provided much scope for obstreperousness. The cosy old box pews were uniquely attached to the major residential properties of the parish, so much so that, if a family were absent, no other persons could use the pew. The poor, unable to afford pew rents even if there were more pews available, could squeeze in only on the far south side of the nave while, at the same time, there could be an almost empty church on the north side.

Giving up the privacy of a household's box pew was a vexed issue and a few placatory measures were adopted: FHM here revealed his enduring characteristics of caution and diplomacy. The policy, as decided by the vestry committee under the leadership of FHM, was that the families in the new pews should occupy the same relative positions as before. Viscount Sydney (later to become Earl Sydney) was opposed to much of what was proposed and resigned from the vestry committee before the work was started. On relinquishing the Frognal pew he was allotted front pews on the north side of what is now the central aisle – one pew still bears the name Sydney.[5]

Similarly, having given up seats in the north gallery, the more co-operative Sir Herbert Jenner-Fust was allotted a long pew on the north side of the nave in lieu of his north gallery seats. Incidentally, Sir Herbert was an example of one of the many distinguished personages who resided in Chislehurst at that time. He lived at Hawkwood, opposite Coopers, and in 1835 was appointed an Ecclesiastical Commissioner charged with looking into ways of remodelling the Church of England. He had been, since 1832, Dean of the Court of Arches, the ecclesiastical court which came into prominence over the celebrated Gorham case from 1847 to 1849.[6] At the end of the case Sir Herbert, frail in health at seventy one years of age, took four and a half months to reach his inevitably controversial decision. To add to the effect he was carried into court by two footmen.

Jenner-Fust had a total of fourteen children. The second and eighth sons, both in Holy Orders, played cricket for Cambridge. Charles Herbert Jenner-Fust combined a career at the Bar with much cricket: he played for England being a particularly successful underhand bowler in the days when round-arm bowling was expressly forbidden. His brother, Henry Lascelles Jenner, became the first Bishop of Dunedin in 1866 but resigned, amid some controversy, in 1871. In their youth, both sons played cricket at Chislehurst. Bishop Jenner, who was at Harrow at the same time as FHM, remained a lifelong friend of Chislehurst and was frequently mentioned in the Parish Magazine as a visiting preacher.

By 1849 the work on the church was finished and it was reconsecrated by Archbishop Sumner on October 23rd, a date which was celebrated at St Nicholas' as a Dedication Festival until the year 1900. In that year it was decided to inaugurate, instead, what would now be called a Patronal Festival i.e. the Feast of St Nicholas on December 6th.

The new arrangements, largely what we see in the present day church, did not escape criticism. The Cambridge Camden Society, formed in 1839 (later to be named the Ecclesiological Society) for the study of ecclesiastical art,[7] aimed at improving standards of ceremonial and advising on Gothic Revival architecture. In their monthly journal, *The Ecclesiologist*, they took it upon themselves to review the many church renovations which were to emerge in the next twenty years or so. About Chislehurst they agreed that the previous box pews were as bad as could be and they welcomed the bench-type pews but commented unfavourably on the provision of doors to the new pews: 'we trust that the existing prejudices in their favour will soon be overcome'.[8] They pronounced that the pew doors were the greatest blemish on the whole undertaking. However, they commented that 'the new aisle will have a pretty open porch of wood'. In summing up they said, somewhat mysteriously: 'The work is not, it will be seen, free from grave faults; but to those who know anything of the parish, it will be a wonder that so much has been done, and in so short a time.'

In his transformed church, FHM started on careful alterations to the worship. When he arrived in 1846 there were two Sunday services with a sermon in the morning only and there were but six Holy Communion services in the whole year. FHM immediately introduced weekday services and monthly Holy Communion. Soon there was to be a more frequent observation of saints' days and also a third evening service on Sundays which was occasionally a Communion service. However, in later years, FHM was to express strong reservations about evening Communion, as did all

Tractarians, because of the impossibility of fasting before receiving.

The first four years of FHM's time in Chislehurst was an episode of vigorous innovation: he was young, inspired and supported by a particularly happy home life. We can only marvel at the efficiency and generosity of FHM and his wife. Their thoughtfulness was to result in what turned out to be an essential arrangement for the next few years.

* * *

Fanny's father was commuting to town daily from Reigate. As another winter arrived John Anderdon, who was not robust, gently informed the family that he felt he could cope no longer with the 'snow and sleet' and the 'frost and rime'. His first thought was that they should all return to live in London but, considerate though his family was, they longed to find a solution that would allow them to remain in the country. The debate reached the ears of 'Franz and Fran'.

> Come all and stay with us awhile,
> we nearer are to Town;
> and easy transit thence have we
> . . . and at the Spring's return
> you may some better plan devise.

The Anderdon family (consisting of mother, father, and three daughters) were persuaded into the happy arrangement and soon were sharing the Murray household's joy at the arrival of a first son, Henry Edward Murray. Anne conjures up a vivid picture of the doting attentions the child commanded:

> Grandmama and Aunties all
> delighted him their own to call,
> vying in joyous chime
> who first each day the darling babe
> should fold within her arms.

When the Anderdons had been there a year they felt they could impose no longer but were pressed to stay for several more months, another baby being on the way.

The happiness of all was now to suffer a devastating blow: in March, a second son, Herbert Francis, was born who cost his mother's life. Fanny died on March 10th, 1850:

> this was a sudden blow
> which shattered all joy.

Francis Murray was, naturally, overwhelmed by this loss. He begged the Anderdon family to stay and help him, not only with the care of the children – a two year old and a new-born baby – but also with the running of his home. Comforting him was an impossibility: all he could do was 'bow his soul beneath the stroke' and brace

The two sons of Francis Murray

by permission of Cdr Nigel Anderdon

himself to perform the many duties of the parish.

The family watched helplessly and after a year or two began gently to suggest that he should think of re-marrying. In 1854, after four years without Fanny, he agreed that this was the right course. Known to the family was Mrs Mary Prescott Saunders who had herself been widowed with small children and, although both broken hearted, they agreed that their similar situations could unite them in a new love. It was rather touchingly written by Anne that

> . . . for a heart
> once given wholly, there was but part
> remaining, while they live,
> but with such part that lady fair
> was pleased to be content.

With the new 'household plan' at the Rectory the Anderdon family needed to rethink their own arrangements but, having cared for Henry and Herbert for four years, they were reluctant to move too far away. The immediate solution was that Anne and Maria should remain in Chislehurst: in Anne's words

> a little empty house we took
> which, crowded well in every nook,
> could us all just contain.

Meanwhile Mr and Mrs Anderdon made a home nearer London for their son John, now working in London, and for their daughter Helen whose education was not yet complete.

* * *

There is just one episode which must be added. In the year after Fanny's death a headstone in the form of a cross was put above Fanny's grave – by the south-east corner of the church. A cross was then a rare sight in a churchyard for the cross, either inside or outside a church, was perceived as a symbol of the Roman Church.[9] 1850 was the year of the re-establishment of the Roman Catholic hierarchy: this was termed an act of Papal Aggression whereby England and Wales were defined by Pope Pius IX as an ecclesiastical province of the Roman Catholic Church. The fact that the Pope referred to the Church of England as 'the Anglican Schism' was provocation indeed and there spread through Great Britain a wave of sectarian indignation. This alone can be the explanation for the vandalism against Fanny's cross: in FHM's own words '...one night the grave cross, then the only one in the churchyard, was wilfully broken in a mistaken anti-zeal of some one person. I left the cross broken for some time, and broken it told for more good even than when it was whole. Afterwards it was so well mended that it would hardly be known to have been broken . . .'[10]

As can be seen by all those who walk along the criss-crossing paths of St Nicholas' churchyard it has, since then, become furnished with many more crosses which, together with the older style tablets, make for lightness and beauty.

'Seldom, if ever, can we find a better example of the beauty with which "God's acre" can be invested, by watchful care guided by good taste.'[11]

---

1 The Rev. Francis Dawson chaired Vestry meetings regularly until April 1842, after which time the curate, Rev. Charles Caffin presided until FHM took regular control in September 1846. Under Dawson the Vestry Room was added to the church, without the connecting passage originally. Dawson personally raised some money towards the costs.

2 Another bequest in FHM's will reads: 'I bequeath the picture of Canterbury Cathedral and the picture of St Nicholas' Church . . . to my successor in the Rectory.'

3 The East window of the South aisle is a memorial to Maria Anderdon, who died in 1904.

4 By introducing pews the seating was increased from 340 places to 530.

5 The 21st century has seen further changes to the pewing at the front and Lord Sydney may have lost his place!

6 The Gorham case was an instance of church and State coming into conflict over a disciplinary matter arising from a doctrinal dispute. This case and its implications are clearly described by Owen Chadwick, *The Victorian Church, part 1.*

7 It has been said that, where the Tractarians *wrote* the Oxford Movement, the Cambridge men *illustrated* it. Christ Church, Kilndown, Kent, was the first church to be furnished and decorated according to the ideals of the Cambridge Camden Society.

8 The hinges can still be seen although the doors are long since gone.

9 In fact, I have not seen a grave cross which predates Fanny's.

10 Webb, Miller and Beckwith, *The History of Chislehurst,* page 89.

11 Archaeologia Cantiana vol. 13 '*Chislehurst and its Church*'.

Chapter 6

Hymns Ancient and Modern[1]
The Development of Congregational Singing

Veni Creator Spiritus

Hymn to the Holy Spirit, ninth century, attributed to RABANUS MAURUS.

If there is one particular aspect of the modern St. Nicholas' Church which has fulfilled and maintained FHM's vision it is the inspiration to worship provided by choir and organ.

The musical development of the church service in general can be charted neatly within the nineteenth century. Taking the year 1800 as a notional starting point, there is just a little known about St Nicholas' Church, but both fact and fiction provide numerous examples of what a country congregation would have had to endure.

During Francis Wollaston's time as Rector (1769-1815) a barrel-organ was introduced and a west gallery had been built in 1785. These facts we know, together with Anne Anderdon's mention of the 'poorly tuned up village band' in the west gallery in 1846. The picture, sketchy though it is, typifies most country churches of the time. Although the West Gallery tradition is now enjoying the attention of musicologists and historians, its role within the church attracted much criticism in the early nineteenth century. Many purists still pine for it but others would say that it has actually made a come-back in some churches in the guise of guitar groups and bands.

Stories abound of the excesses of the 'Dad's Army' of musicians at the back of the rural church. The situation so easily lends itself to exaggeration that it is wisest to quote from what one hopes is an honest source. Here, from the pages of the periodical *The Parish Choir*[2] (1848) 'an old singer' describes a typical West Gallery contribution to the service: 'On assembling (often after the service has begun) there is the How d'ye do? What are we to have today? How did people say the hymn went last Sunday evening? and similar gossip to be discussed. The books are to be found and sorted; Mr A. must be told to mind such a point, where the tenor leads; Mr B. cautioned not to sing too loud, etc. Mr C. has not got a part; so a leaf must be torn out of one of the music books, and it must be copied with a pencil; so they sit and crouch together, holding a whispering chat till the time comes for the grand display. Then curtains are withdrawn; they come forward and sing their parts. The psalm over, the curtains are closed: and they sit down again and criticise the thing they have just done. Thus the time is beguiled until the next psalm; then follows the sermon, when one or two shirk out; others sit and sleep or talk or peep between the curtains at the ladies in the congregation.[3]

'In fact, the occupants of these galleries do not, for the most part, come to praise God or to pray; they come to sing, either for the gratification of a musical taste, or for the gratification of vanity, or for pay . . . As for leading the congregation, it is the last thing your gallery singers dream of. They ridicule the idea; and render the thing as impossible as they can.'

No doubt they were correct here when Church music, by ecclesiastical ruling, was confined to the rendition of psalms, allowable as scriptural texts. The West Gallery tunes were in four parts, fugal in style, much ornamented and famously ill-fitted to the words.[4] An additional bar to congregational participation was the fact that the tune was held by the tenor line. The West Gallery singers, with their instruments, viewed their contribution as a performance: the congregation sat politely through this. But even in the absence of a band the congregation's plight was often no better. The Parish Clerk laboriously intoned the sung parts of the service and there was a system of 'lining out' the psalms which was tedious and lengthy: a psalm, sung line by line by the clerk and repeated by the congregation, could take as long as a full hour by this method!

* * *

At this time, people were not used to singing in church, nor was there a local choral tradition. It was only at the beginning of Victoria's reign that musicians tackled the problem and this, surprisingly, happened under a government initiative: the intention had more to do with morals than music. The musician who was invited to transform the nation's singing was John Hullah, organist of Croydon Parish Church. He had studied techniques for the teaching of singing to massed assemblies and after 1840, thousands of schoolmasters, having attended classes in London's Exeter Hall, went back to their schools equipped to pass on the elements of good singing to their pupils. In July 1842 the number of people attending the classes was computed at fifty thousand. The importance of school singing, both in Public Schools and local schools (such as St Nicholas' School, Chislehurst, at a later date) continued for more than a century.

It was hardly surprising that a thirst for hymn singing was beginning to emerge, especially as the Wesleyans and Congregationalists, to name but two groups of hymn-singing non-conformists, had been singing hymns for decades. It was at about this time that the new brand of clergy, Tractarians like FHM, cascaded into village churches across the country.[5] Like FHM they set about making changes which would facilitate devotion and concentration. Tactfully, or not so tactfully, the village bands were dispensed with.[6] In many places it would seem that the band aimed at controlling the service and earlier clergy had become helpless. The determined Tractarian clergyman was in a new category.

In spite of the fact that hymns in the form of non-Biblical poetical compositions were not authorised in the Church of England, hymn books were beginning to emerge on a parish by parish basis. And here, for once, Tractarian and Evangelical were equally keen although the taste for the same hymns was not always shared.

When FHM arrived in Chislehurst they were using Tate and Brady, the *New Version of the Psalms* which had been published in 1696! It was sometimes bound and printed together with the *Book of Common Prayer* which was the equivalent of a seal of official approval. However, in the days of Wollaston's barrel organ there had been a collection, produced in 1803, *Psalms and Hymns for use of the Parish Church of Chislehurst*: the barrel organ had been capable of churning out as many as thirty six tunes.

FHM clearly wanted to set about the music question as soon as he came to Chislehurst. Bearing in mind the tremendous activity on the fabric of the church and the upheaval of his circumstances caused by Fanny's death, it is surprising that he was able to produce a hymn book so soon – though he was helped by collaboration with his curate, the Rev. C. Harrison. *A Hymnal for Use in the English Church* came out in 1852. This is a charming little book, very comfortable to hold (4" x 6" x ½"), with navy blue, embossed binding and displaying on the front page the words, 'Joy and gladness shall be found therein, thanksgiving and the voice of melody'. It was printed by John and Charles Mozley.[7] It sold for 6d and the compilers gave up all profit. The names of the editors appeared nowhere in the book: it was only in later editions that owners had written in the name of Francis Murray in ink – no mention of Harrison. The book was enormously successful and after only three editions it had already sold 20,000 copies; by 1869 there had been thirteen editions. Part I consists of Hymns for the Week; Part II Hymns proper for the Holy Seasons and Holy Days; Part III is a collection of non-specific hymns. There are very many there that are still sung today: for example, 'On Jordan's bank', 'Brightest and Best', 'Sun of my Soul', etc. In the whole book there were originally 158 hymns, increasing to 293 by the last edition. In deference to the Church's ruling[8] on hymns the compilers used many ancient hymns translated from the Latin, claiming that they had earned a legitimate place by their early usage. Each hymn was headed by an appropriate Biblical quotation – another device for ensuring that it passed muster. Included were some of John Wesley's hymns and one of them illustrates the sort of change that was made: 'Jesu, Lover of my Soul' became 'Jesu, Refuge of my Soul'. As examples of new material, John Keble's verses from *The Christian Year* appeared frequently. However, as well as anonymity on the matter of editors there was a silence about the sources of the hymns. The reasoning was that a book for worship must be for the glory of God, not man.

* * *

It was in the summer of 1858 that the next and most famous stage of FHM's interest in hymnody began – in a Great Western Railway carriage. In the preface to his own 1852 hymnal there had appeared the thought: 'The editors hope the hymnal may in some measure meet a generally acknowledged want and be a step towards that which they still hope for, a Hymnal possessing the same authority of the Church as the Book of Common Prayer.' It would seem that FHM and his companion, the Rev. William Denton, (editor of *The Church Hymnal*, 1853) were in conversation on this very topic, for they resolved during the course of their railway journey to gather together other interested parties and work on the idea of producing just one collection containing all that was best from the current explosion in hymnals. The proposal was that all those who had produced their own hymnals should surrender them to this ideal. The railway carriage conversation was, of course, the impetus for the development of *Hymns Ancient and Modern*.

The fact that this resolution was proposed in a railway carriage, of all places, was a fitting tribute to the emerging railway system which, over the next few years, was going to transport enthusiastic clergymen backwards and forwards on miles of *A&M* business. Credit goes also to the Post Office, itself dependent on the railways, for conveying thousands of letters between clergy in parishes scattered over England and Wales.[9] At the Canterbury Press in Norwich there are acres of closely handwritten pages, often illegible.

As soon as they could, Murray and Denton convened a meeting which took place at St Barnabas', Pimlico, where the Rev. George Cosby White had just been made Curate in Charge. George Cosby White had been a Curate under FHM in Chislehurst, (1853-1857). They brought in also, amongst others, the Rev. Henry Baker, Vicar of Monkland in Herefordshire (who in 1859, succeeded to his father's Baronetcy) and it was he who became the overall editor of *Hymns Ancient and Modern*.

Their first action was to put an advertisement in *The Guardian*[10] in October 1858: 'To the clergy and others interested in hymnology. The Editors of several existing hymnals being engaged, with others, in the compilation of a book which they hope may secure a more general acceptance from churchmen, would be thankful for any suggestions from persons interested in the matter.' The advertisement unleashed a frenzy of activity: at one stroke clergymen, particularly those in country parishes, were drawn into a vast and exciting enterprise in which they could participate. Isolated incumbents, earnestly doing their best for their little flocks, were now absorbed into a whirl of sociability – by letter and by train. Those who could sent in their own local hymnals and many submitted their own compositions. There was a mania for translating Latin and German texts and church organists had a heyday, setting old and new hymns to music. Material poured in, it was passed around for comment, criticised, altered and polished up to fit the desired style. The aim was that the hymns should teach the truths of the faith expressed in impeccable wording and set to tunes that were within a musical range suitable for congregational singing. The real achievement of *A&M* was the successful marriage of excellent words with an excellent tune. This must surely be the definition of 'a fine hymn'. Take for example, the words of 'Abide with me' by H. F. Lyte[11] (1847) with its setting 'Eventide' by W. H. Monk. There *is* another tune but could there be a better match than the familiar one? The idea was that frequent singing of the hymn to the same well-loved tune would engrave the words and message on the singer's soul.

After the first flurry of activity the organisation for publishing *A&M* evolved into a committee of thirteen proprietors who had each put up money for the venture – FHM was one of these. This was an independent committee and was not authorised by the Church: this status they valued as it gave them more freedom. The networking continued and consultation over minutiae was a serious business, a team of academic theologians and literary experts being on hand to give opinions. The publication was powered by working clergymen – its strength was in the co-operation at grass roots level and the common aims of all concerned. The fact that all were united spiritually made, on the whole, for courtesy and happiness in the task. Each meeting began with the words of '*Veni Creator Spiritus*' and this became a tradition. The clergymen enjoyed their gatherings: 'I will promise not to drench you with cider or ginger beer as I did last time'[12] conjures up a scene of clerical levity in the Rectory garden.

A&M was published in 1861 and FHM was involved with the whole process. This inevitably meant a great many meetings and much absence from the parish. FHM had other reasons for being absent (Chapter 9) and even before the *A&M* project John Anderdon had written, in 1857: 'I wish he would keep to his own parish and not go scampering up to town to attend meetings so much – his people are not the better for it.'

FHM was, as has already been mentioned, a proprietor who had made an investment and, judging from the letters in the archives, he was an active committee worker. However, he was not himself a composer of hymns or tunes but he did bring to the project his own experience in compiling a hymnal. His duties seem to have included 'making apologies' and 'writing placatory letters'. For all that the essence of *A&M* meetings and correspondence was pleasant and professional the inevitable differences of opinion and misunderstandings had to be confronted and FHM, though not necessarily successful at making peace, was adept at penning a firm but apologetic letter.

In 1862 he was writing to William Denton. It would seem that, although a participant in the famous inaugural railway carriage conversation, William Denton had given his colleagues to understand that he was not prepared to forgo his interest in his own hymnbook: he was now complaining that he had been left out of everything. Perhaps a mistake had been made in omitting to inform him of an important meeting but, wrote FHM, 'I myself undertook to go to you in the City early the following morning to try and get you to our next meeting. I went and to my astonishment and regret found you were not prepared to join us but intended to adhere to your own book . . . sorely disappointed . . . had very much desired your co-operation . . . I did think you had backed out of it . . . I am sincerely sorry . . . I don't wish to throw vinegar on the past but I can only state my own distinct recollection in vindication of myself and others . . .'

One can see that this was a most unfortunate matter. However, it does highlight one of the problems of bringing out *A&M* – what to do about the proliferation of books already in circulation. Withdrawing further editions at short notice would be a great inconvenience and expense to parishes and anyway congregations would probably have a loyalty to their local hymnbooks. FHM's Chislehurst book, having sold so many copies, could hardly have been called a local book and he allowed many editions to go ahead. Its eventual fate is quite interesting. By 1866 the book is appearing with a tune for each hymn, looking very much like *A&M*, but very clearly the product not of Francis Murray, but of the Hon. and Rev. John Grey, Rector of Houghton le Spring, between Durham and Sunderland.

The fact that the new editor was an 'Honourable' prompts the observation that the Tractarian clergy of the day were noticeably 'well born'. FHM himself (Chapter 1) came from a ducal family but researching his clerical associates yields many titles and distinguished families. The Hon. and Rev. John Grey, for example, was a son of the

2nd Earl Grey, the Whig Prime Minister whose ministry was responsible for the Reform Act of 1832.[13]

Another example of clergy tetchiness came from the Dean of Canterbury, Henry Alford. In October 1864 he had complained in a letter to *The Guardian* that his harvest hymn, 'Come, ye thankful people, come' had been included without permission in *A&M*: what is more, it had been altered. Within a few days, FHM wrote to him: 'I think you have forgotten the fact that when I was at Canterbury . . . at the installation of the Archbishop, I apologised to you on behalf of the committee of the *Hymns Ancient and Modern,* for having taken the hymn without asking your consent, stating that they had only recently been made aware that it was yours'. FHM reported back his progress with Alford, including the words: 'I was not commissioned to say anything about alterations . . .' which somewhat confirms the suspicion that dealing with complaints was FHM's allotted task. Faced with Dean Alford's intransigence[14] and his refusal to acknowledge publicly that he had received an apology the proprietors were 'in a fix now as to continuing the hymn as it is'. This was not resolved until 1871 with the death of Henry Alford when, with telling haste, his widow wrote to the proprietors of *A&M* allowing the use of the hymn.[15] The flavour of the letter suggested that she had had no patience with her late husband's stance.

* * *

In spite of many criticisms *A&M* sold and sold and sold, gradually replacing the build-up of local hymn books. It was by no means appreciated by all, particularly as it was very much a product of the Oxford Movement: James Ormiston, the vicar of Old Hill, Dudley, expressed his thoughts by means of a pamphlet entitled '*Hymns Ancient and Modern* and their Romanising Tendency'. However, others criticised the inclusion of evangelical hymns of a personal and sentimental nature.

By 1894 *A&M* was being used in 70% of churches as well as being taken up by schools, the armed services and, most significantly, in private homes. No self-respecting Victorian family would be without a few copies of *A&M* for singing round the piano. The first edition, without music, sold 4.5 million copies in the first eight years and when the music edition came out in 1889, a million copies were dispersed on the day of publication. The music edition was still without information on writers and composers: this development came only in 1922.

Such success inevitably brought in a good income for the proprietors who, on the whole, put the proceeds into appropriate projects. For Chislehurst, the happy consequence of the *A&M* bonanza was the Church of the Annunciation to the Blessed Virgin Mary (Chapter 11). Referring to the funds arising from his interest in *A&M* FHM wrote: 'These I placed at the disposal of the church, and through the great and increasing success of the book I was happily enabled to devote a considerable sum by degrees towards the amount required for the completion of the church'.[16] He also paid the stipend of the assistant clergy for many years, until new arrangements were made.

At The Annunciation, as also at St Nicholas', the choir was a strong feature. At St Nicholas', only the boys wore cassocks by 1868, the men had succumbed by 1880.

The reason for the delay was explained by FHM: 'The want of uniformity is accounted for by the unwillingness of the men to adopt the cassock: but it was not thought well to lose their kind assistance by making the adoption of so decent and proper a habit as an absolute rule. Perhaps all will see their way eventually to conform to ecclesiastical usage.'[17] And indeed this did happen: the choir photograph of 1891 shows thirty-two men, boys and clergy posed in cassocks and surplices outside the vestry door.

* * *

There is just one footnote to the *A&M* story as it applies to FHM: it illustrates his kindness and his status as a person from whom to seek help. William Henry Monk (1823-1889) was the musical editor of *A&M* which, by the time of his death, had sold 30 million copies: he had just sent to press the 1889 edition when he died. He was a parish organist, not one of the proprietors, and had no share in the profits. On the erection of a memorial cross to him in Highgate Cemetery (this had been initiated and followed through by FHM) there was to be issued the customary subscription list but some had wanted to publish with this list the details of the annuity (another of FHM's initiatives) that the proprietors had granted to Monk's widow, Hope Isidora Monk. FHM mobilised like-minded friends to support the exclusion of this material which would perhaps have been a humiliation for Mrs Monk and her daughter. In one of her letters to FHM she describes the writing of the tune to 'Abide with me': 'That was written at a time of great sorrow. Hand in hand we were silently watching the glory of the setting sun until the golden hue faded – then he took paper, and pencilled the tune which has gone all over the world.'

A fitting finale to the amazing story of *Hymns Ancient and Modern*. By the end of FHM's life in 1902 *A&M* was a national institution and, in the luggage of pioneering missionaries, had travelled throughout the empire.

'As o'er each continent and island
The dawn leads on another day,
The voice of prayer is never silent
Nor dies the strain of praise away.

So be it, Lord; Thy throne shall never
Like earth's proud empires pass away:
Thy Kingdom stands and grows for ever,
Till all Thy creatures own Thy sway.'[18]

---

1 I have drawn heavily on the following sources for this chapter: *Abide with Me* by Ian Bradley and *The Historical Companion to Hymns Ancient and Modern* edited by Maurice Frost. I wish to thank the Canterbury Press, Norwich, for generously allowing me to work at the *Ancient and Modern* archives.

2 Quoted by Ian Bradley in *Abide With Me*. Unfortunately, the style and vocabulary of the quotation suggest some doctoring of 'the old singer's' words.

3 Another source (Woods, *Good Singing Still*) suggests that card-playing was a diversion during the sermon. However, in retaliation, some clergy took to the vestry during the singing of the psalms.

4 See Dean Hole's example in Chapter 4.

5 For a detailed survey of the impact of Tractarians on the Churches of Kent see Nigel Yates, *Kent and the Oxford Movement.*

6 Thomas Hardy is a good source for many references to the West Gallery tradition: *Under the Greenwood Tree* in particular.

7 Two more brothers, Thomas and James were actively involved with the Oxford Movement. Thomas married Harriet, the sister of John Henry Newman.

8 Hymns were not fully accepted as part of Anglican worship until the Lincoln Judgement of Archbishop Benson in 1890 by which the use of hymns was allowed as long as they did not interrupt the course of the service.

9 Scotland is omitted deliberately. The Church of Scotland clung for much longer to the exclusive singing of metrical Psalms.

10 A weekly religious newspaper founded in 1846 to uphold Tractarian principles and to show their relevance to the best secular thought of the day.

11 'Abide with me' was written in the year of Lyte's death: another of his hymns was 'Praise, my soul, the King of Heaven'. He had struggled against ill-health for many years and his death took place in Nice where he was hoping to recuperate. He is buried in the English Cemetery there.

12 Letter from FHM to Henry Baker.

13 He is perhaps even better remembered as having given his name to a certain type of China Tea.

14 Also, dare it be said, a little venom. 'I hope that that this one case is not a sample of the small care with which search for the originals and authors was made.'

15 Other hymns by Henry Alford include 'Ten thousand times ten thousand' and 'In token that thou shalt not fear'.

16 Webb, Miller and Beckwith, *The History of Chislehurst.*

17 Parish Magazine: March 1868.

18 Two verses of the hymn 'The day Thou gavest, Lord, is ended'. The words were by John Ellerton but its inseparable tune, St Clement, although attributed to the Rev. Clement Cotterill Scholefield is thought to have been improved by the hand of Sir Arthur Sullivan.

Chapter 7

Fire at the Parish Church

My Dear Parishioners,

Many of you have kindly expressed a wish to read the Sermon which was preached before the destruction of the steeple, with so little thought of what was to follow; and the Sermon addressed to you after that sad calamity. I have, therefore committed them to print, and trust that they may prove some memorial both of the love and mercy which we have so undeservedly received, and of our duty when the danger is past.

Your affectionate Friend and Pastor,

FRANCIS H. MURRAY

March 26th, 1857

For the morning of Sunday, March 15th FHM had prepared a particularly outspoken sermon. His sermons were prepared meticulously, written out in full, and so for his sermons to be printed and distributed was a relatively easy matter: these two sermons have been stored in the British Library and the Bodleian since 1857.

In his obituary in the Westminster Gazette the following comment was made: 'He was no preacher as far as eloquence was concerned, but few gave more instruction in their sermons and he lived down opposition by the sheer force of his high character and his transparent earnestness.' An understanding of what is here meant by 'eloquence' can only be speculation – perhaps the writer of the obituary meant that FHM did not deliver his sermon *extempore*. The contrary view is that it is possible to speak more effectively from a prepared text.

The sermon of March 15th (which would have lasted for at least half an hour) was a call to the parishioners to take their church and their worship more seriously. He started in a general way, deploring the 'frightful unconcern and irreverence' seen so often in churches. He spoke of 'the dumbness, and the deadness of prayer and praise which is the fault of so many congregations'.

His next point seemed to be addressed more directly to the people in front of him: 'How can we, any of us, neglect or insult that Blessed Saviour by wandering eye and wandering thoughts, and careless, unkneeling attitudes! Would any of us thus treat the abodes of earthly royalty?'

He finally made it clear that it was the people of St. Nicholas' who were in the firing line. 'My brethren, how is it that some of you seem so cold in prayer, that some of you, whom I could name and point to in this church, seem to take but little part with us and some even sit in prayer as though they said "We have no part in this matter"… Why not kneel when you pray?' He then reminded them that on Good Friday, in the Collect, the whole Church prays for 'Jews, Turks, Infidels and Hereticks'. He pointed out to them: 'If a Turk were to come into a Christian Church, and see you *sitting* while prayer was offered, he would say "Do you call this Christian worship? Do you desire to teach *me*? It is one of the first and strictest rules of my religion, to kneel in prayer."'

Further criticism followed: 'Let me explain what is meant by kneeling. It is not leaning forward and putting the head down . . . It is not even kneeling upon the knees and resting back against the seat . . . but to kneel forward, simply and fully upon the knees, reverently using the arms and raising the hands'.

He then addressed the matter of responses: 'Why is there so little voice raised in supplication? . . . Do try and remedy this coldness; do try and speak out fully with your voice; do endeavour to pray and praise, and sing with a full heart and open mouth'.

He concluded with an exhortation to more attendance at weekday services or, at least, to the cultivation of a habit of calling in at the open church for private prayer.[1] This last plea was illustrated with the example of peasants in other lands whom he had seen, on their way to market, putting down their baskets in the church porch while they offered up their morning prayer.

Prophetically he finished: 'My brethren, I have spoken to you in plain words. A time will come which will prove to each soul whether they are important or not'. FHM can hardly have expected a significant event in the Parish so soon.

* * *

On Monday 16th March, 1857, fire broke out at the church. FHM recorded the details in *The History of Chislehurst.*

There were six bells in the church at that time, rung from the middle stage of the tower, and to deaden the sound, sacking had been put under the bells. The conclusion as to the cause of the fire was that on the Sunday afternoon a man, who was known to have been up in the tower looking out for 'his mate coming from Prickend', must have dropped a match on the sacking. It must have smouldered for several hours.

There was nothing untoward at the end of the evening service; at 10pm a woman on a passing omnibus saw a light but thought nothing of it; at 4am a passing sweep observed nothing when he looked up at the clock. However, at 5.30am the alarm was raised when 'a little smoke like a puff from a tobacco pipe' could be seen emerging from the top of the spire. The Church Clerk was first woken up and then the Rector who was now greeted by the sight of a 'black volume of smoke issuing from the base of the spire'. The Rector was soon on the spot directing operations with Mr Wollaston, a churchwarden. They called all who could to help, 'some going for buckets and ladders, some for the engine at Frognal and some for the parish engine'. When the engines arrived it was too late to save the spire and the most terrifying part was to hear the bells crashing to the base of the tower. Mr Wollaston advised that water from a small garden engine should be played onto the burning timbers as they fell and this prevented the nearby pews from catching fire. Fortunately, the direction of the wind had changed from the previous day, otherwise, the church would itself would have been in great danger. It was certainly a village effort: 'A double line was formed to convey water to the engines and for the return of the empty buckets and two-thousand bucketsful were obtained from the wells of the houses to the north of the church'.

At noon on the day of the fire a *Te Deum* was offered as a thanksgiving for the escape from a greater evil, that is, the destruction of the whole church. The tower was boarded off and the services took place as usual on the Sunday following.

In the course of his account of the fire FHM thought that two happenings were rather extraordinary. The wife of the Church Clerk, at some time of the night, woke him saying the church was on fire but he, confident that he had locked up safely, merely said 'my dear, you are only dreaming' and turning round, went to sleep again. Three quarters of a mile away, Admiral Harding was uneasy and thought there was fire about: 'He asked Mrs Harding to get up and look round; she did so, but found nothing'. No doubt, after that assurance, the Admiral also turned round and went to sleep again!

In his sermon on the next Sunday FHM used the opportunity to push home the message that it was only through God's mercy that the church had been saved, not because the people of Chislehurst, himself included, deserved such a deliverance. 'It will make us love and care for it more and use it more reverently . . . I cannot forbear to allude with great thankfulness to the order, and quiet, and reverence which was pointedly noticed as such a striking feature amid all the distress and perplexity.' He rounded off with a call for more church attendance: 'There are many whom we see here only in hours of danger, or at funerals, or some such public occasions but who, unhappily, do not form a body of devout and regular worshippers'.

* * *

CHISLEHURST CHURCH.

The church after 1857

Within days of the fire, plans were under way for the rebuilding. At the restoration committee meeting on April 23rd Mr George Wollaston's[2] offer to act as architect, without fee, was formally accepted. Some questions needed to be settled. For example: had there originally been battlements on the tower around the base of the spire? Mr George Edmund Street (1824-1881), a well known ecclesiastical architect, was of the opinion that there had been and he favoured restoring the tower to the original designer's plan of four hundred years ago. Mr Wollaston thought the parishioners would like the tower to look as it had done just before the fire. However, he did raise the height of the tower by four feet because of the internal difficulty at the top of the stair and he also raised the spire itself by four feet. Both before and after the fire the height of the tower equalled the height of the spire. Together with the new weathervane the total increase in height was eleven feet five inches.

The bells, with their 'strong English oak frame', were increased in number from six to eight and the ringing chamber was brought down to its present ground floor position. Eighteen months after the fire, when the bellfounders Messrs Warner and Sons had completed the work, 'eight members of the St James's Society of London paid a visit to Chiselhurst (sic) and rang upon the bells of the Parish Church . . . They cannot be surpassed by any peal of their weight (tenor 17cwt) in the country.'[3]

photograph by Frank Draper

The Cockerel from the spire of the church when regilded in 1957

The new weathervane was the now familiar golden cockerel. The illustration shows the cockerel when it was brought down for repair and regilding in 1957.[4] The replacement of the simple cross which can be seen on old drawings of the church was not discussed at the Vestry meetings. However, that the subject should be a cockerel was not, I suspect, because of the proximity to the Cockpit on the common but because the cockerel announces that darkness has vanished and light has come. The bird, when set on high, symbolises the supremacy in human life of the spiritual. Not everyone was in favour of the cockerel. John Anderdon, in a letter to a friend wrote: 'The spire is finished and the weathercock come down [from the maker] *fully* larger – but the cross fixed on, veered about with every wind (not of doctrine) which we all at once thought objectionable . . . I did not like the idea of the emblem of St Peter being the resting place of the cross'.

The 1858 clock makes for an interesting feature of the church. The clock mechanism is to the same design as that of Big Ben, the clock in St Stephen's Tower, Westminster, and indeed was in place a year before Big Ben. The design was the work of the then Edmund Becket Denison (1816-1905), later to be created the first Baron Grimthorpe.

Until the end of the century the Dedication of the renewed church was celebrated on a date near to October 20th and 'celebrate' has to be understood in its fullest sense. The essential element was a procession[5] before the church service, a visiting preacher and then a sit-down meal for around four hundred in the Parish Room. After 1870 the Dedication Festival was enhanced in that it had been organised that the Church of the Annunciation, dedicated in that year, should share the same day.

1 According to J. Embry, *The Catholic Movement and SSC*, St. Nicholas' was one of the first churches to be kept open for private devotion. Normally it was open from 10 to 5 but FHM was happy to extend or change the times if desired.

2 Churchwarden, architect and grandson of Francis Wollaston LLB, Rector of Chislehurst from 1769-1815.

3 From a letter signed 'A Lover of Church Bells' addressed to the Editor of *The Sun*. The first peal by a Chislehurst band did not take place until 1864.

4 The work was carried out by J.W. Gray and Son Ltd: the steeplejack was Mr A. Wallbridge of Salisbury.

5 In 1867, for example, the procession consisted of the clergy of the parish, the choir and 27 other clergy. They left the vestry, processed through the churchyard and entered by the West Door.

Chapter 8

The Anderdon Family

To pray or omit a prayer, to restrain the tongue or give it way, to curb temper or yield to it: these things tell silently but surely on our eternal state.

WILLIAM ANDERDON

The Anderdon family should have a central place in any book about Victorian Chislehurst and its Rector. They represent the kind of gentlefolk who made up the backbone of Chislehurst society: well-educated, generous and with church-centred lives. FHM married into the Anderdon family, a tragically short marriage as it turned out, and then for four years the ladies of the family nursed and cared for the two young Murray sons, Henry Edward and Herbert Francis. This was until FHM's remarriage in 1854. Unforeseen deaths were such a feature of Victorian times that fortunes moved around unexpectedly and a later twist to the story will bring FHM's elder son, Henry, back into the family. And, just as in any typical nineteenth century novel, fortunes are made and fortunes are lost and thus it was for the Anderdons.

Another aspect of the family that places it well and truly in the nineteenth century is the enthusiasm for the Tractarian cause: the Anderdons are representative of those families who suffered when loved ones were swept off on the wave of secessions to Rome.

by permission of Cdr Nigel Anderdon

John Anderdon

John Lavicount Anderdon (1792-1874) was from a Somerset family: the church at Ruishton, near Taunton, contains memorials to many generations of Anderdons. He was born in Bristol and attended Harrow School. As a young man he was living at his father's newly built house in Westminster, just a few doors away from the town house of William Manning MP who was, for a while, the wealthy Governor of the Bank of England. John Anderdon struck up a friendship with Frederick, the second son of William Manning, and the two young men went into business with him – trading lucratively in the West Indies. In Anne Anderdon's words 'these were the palmy days'. William Manning's position and wealth enabled him to entertain the rich and important of the day including, according to Anne, the Duke of Wellington. His main residence was Combe Bank, near Sundridge, Kent.

Involvement with the Manning family was significant in other ways. John assumed the role of mentor to Frederick's much younger brother, Henry Edward (1808-1892), later to be Cardinal Manning, Archbishop of Westminster. This was to

Manning and Anderdon

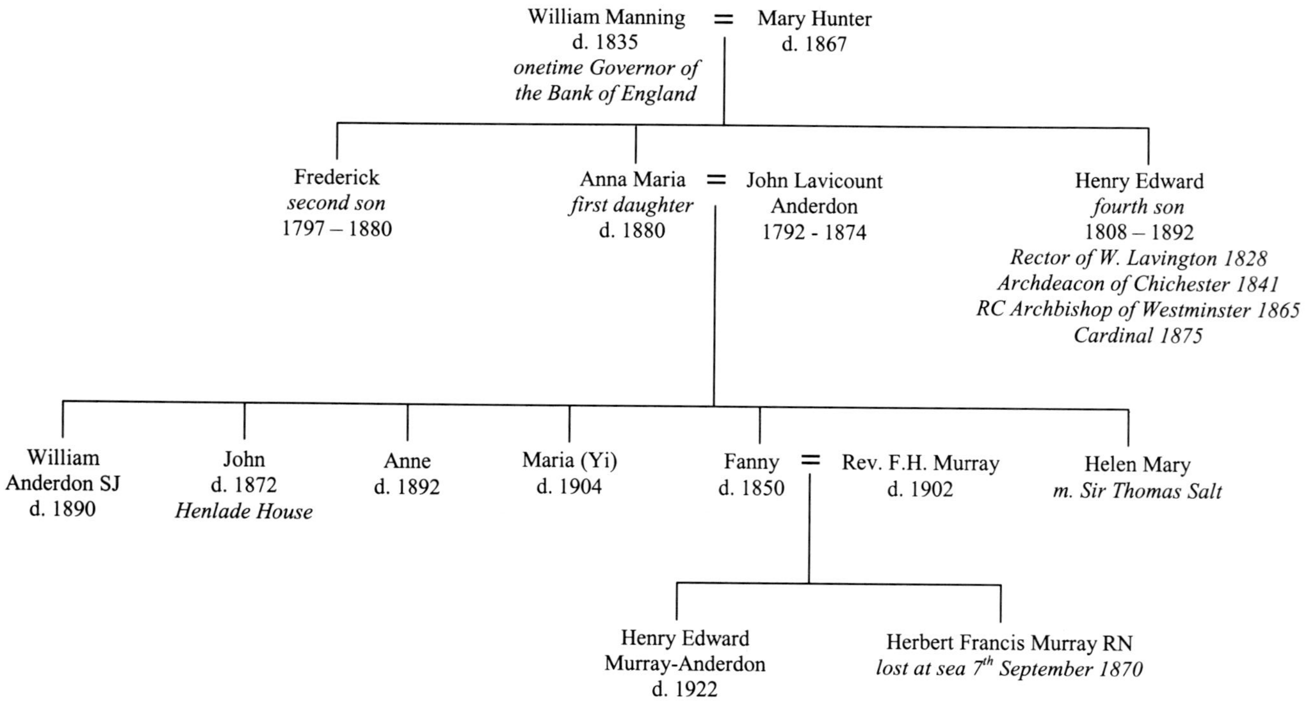

This pedigree shows only those family members mentioned in the text

be, in due course, a source of both pride and sorrow. Yet more importantly, in 1816 John married Frederick's sister, Anna Maria. Thus were the Manning[1] and Anderdon families united.

But before the marriage had taken place, a chest complaint brought John Anderdon to bed:

> Physicians of those older days
> Phlebotomy approved
> and so to him with lancet came
> and too freely bled his weakened frame.

To put the matter right it seemed essential that he should spend some time in a warmer climate: what better than that John should visit the plantations in the West Indies?

There was another reason for this, apart from John Anderdon's health. The Slave Trade had recently been abolished (1807) and William Wilberforce was agitating to enforce the bolder step of giving freedom to the slaves (1833). The Mannings and Anderdons were not alone in accepting that slavery was morally and theologically justifiable. Indeed it was thought to be in the best interests of slaves to be managed in this way. The Manning-Anderdon business partnership and their families were anxious to verify that the seemingly exaggerated descriptions of the horrors of life on the plantations were untrue: at least in the case of their own trading links. They cannot be blamed entirely for not supporting the Evangelical crusade against slavery for this was still a radical movement. However, the fact that the Manning and Anderdon partnership suffered unease is a tribute to their sensibilities. In general, people were convinced that only 'negroes' could work on the sugar plantations; that they were essential; that if slaves were treated well they could hardly wish for more. Indeed, this paternalistic view was confirmed by John Anderdon's observations for he could detect no discontent while in the West Indies. He sent home an enthusiastic account of the warmth of welcome from the slaves and their genuine wish to please him. He praised also the management of the estates and the fair treatment.

Back in England, the business partners were relieved to hear John Anderdon's report. Their conclusion was that what slaves now needed was education, particularly of a Christian nature, and from the family's point of view there seemed no reason why the business should not flourish as ever. On the strength of this confidence and John Anderdon's restored health, his marriage with Anna Maria took place.

The confidence in continued prosperity was misplaced. Slavery as it had existed became unmanageable and threatened by competition from the French and the Americans after the end of the Napoleonic Wars; more specifically, it was the opinion of at least one other West India merchant that Manning and Anderdon did not adequately supervise their estates.[2] The upshot of these misfortunes was the collapse of the merchant firm and in 1831 the three partners found themselves in the bankruptcy court. William Manning, having enjoyed high office as well as wealth, suffered the humiliation of laying down his watch and seals as tokens of his last

by permission of Cdr Nigel Anderdon

Left to right: Maria, Helen, Mrs Anderdon, Anne

possessions.[3] William Manning, thereafter a broken man, died in 1835 and was buried at Combe Bank.

* * *

The sudden poverty of both families had a particularly punishing effect on Henry Edward Manning who was nearing the end of his time at Oxford, a glittering star of the newly formed Oxford Union and apparently destined for an equally glittering career as a politician. For many years he had carried on a correspondence with John Anderdon who was like an elder brother to him. Although John Anderdon provided an invaluable training in literary style and furnished his *protégé* with inspiring book lists it was not a correspondence which unfailingly added lustre to the memory of either of them. John Anderdon, loveable but garrulous, could produce many a didactic platitude which tried the patience of the arrogant, young Henry Edward[4] at Oxford. He, in turn, was well capable of responding with youthful impertinence. However, the relationship survived these acid moments and John Anderdon always referred to Manning as 'my dear boy'. Henry Edward, now with no financial backing, could not hope for entry into parliament and had to settle for the Church: in contrast Gladstone, Manning's sparring partner at the Oxford Union, altered *his* original plan to go into the Church in order to become a politician.

Manning's story had interesting twists. Like Newman, he started life as an Evangelical but gradually came round to the Tractarian view. His abilities ensured rapid progress[5] in the Church of England but his personal life was dogged by tragedy.

He had married, in 1833, one of the four daughters of the Rector of Lavington whom he succeeded later that year. After four happy years Caroline died, having caught a chill while out visiting a sick parishioner. In 1849, unhappy, unwell and disillusioned with the Church of England, particularly after the Gorham judgement, Manning took time off to see Rome: the result, even though he was later to say that he had found the Roman Catholic services highly repulsive, was an increasing Romanisation of his own parish and a rush to Rome from his own flock. In April 1851 he also was received into the Church of Rome. It is difficult for the people of today to imagine the horror of this for the family.

However, for the Anderdon family this was a second blow. John Anderdon's first son, William Henry, who at the time of the wedding of Francis and Fanny was Curate at St Laurence's, Reigate, had been received into the Church of Rome in November 1850. By then he was Vicar of St Margaret's with Knighton, Leicester. William was a brilliant scholar and in spite of the family's impoverished circumstances it had always been agreed that William's education should be a priority: at about the age of fifteen he began to attend classes at King's College, London, and finally graduated from Balliol College, Oxford, in 1839. Informing his father of his decision to leave the Church of England he expressed great distress and a fear that he was permanently offending him. That a family should experience this twice over was no unusual occurrence: as another example, three of the four sons of William Wilberforce went over to Rome.[6] There was a torrent of able men, and women, leaving the Church of England. 'The religious mood of the age, a mood of reaction and romance and feeling and poetry, drew educated men and women towards Catholicism.'[7]

Anne describes the effect on her father, now aged nearly 60:

> The loss of these two dear ones was a blow
> from which my father's aching heart and brow
> recovered scantly for a lengthened space.
> The gathering storm had so come on apace
> that in advancing years he scarce could face
> such keen and rapid, deeply searching woe.

A further knock for John Anderdon came in 1872 when William announced that he was to take the vows of the Society of Jesus. This act, as well as wounding his own father, led to the development of an unpleasant correspondence between William and his uncle who had, by now, been made Archbishop of Westminster. Since childhood, William had loved and admired his Uncle Henry who responded with useful support by appointing him as his secretary from 1856 until 1872. However, Manning showed contempt of Jesuits and accusatory letters from William Anderdon in 1872 exposed Manning, in his turn, to the hurt of receiving impertinent letters from a *protégé*. Perhaps he recognised himself for he displayed forbearance in the face of his nephew's attack.[8]

William Anderdon's life in the Roman Catholic Church in effect removed him from the family home, promoting John, the younger brother, to be heir in his place. (John was the brother to whom Anne addressed her poem.) John's inheritance would be much diminished as a result of his father's bankruptcy and prolonged struggle to rise again. Anne's poem and letters are suffused with concern at her father's daily travel to an office in London and the effect of this upon his health.

* * *

The younger John, after Eton and Oxford, took up a business career but in middle age enjoyed a change of fortune in that Henlade House, the Anderdon family home near Taunton, came to him by the death of the then owner. However, Henlade, built in the 1820s, had never flourished as a family home: no child had ever been born and raised at the house since it was built and it had never passed directly from father to son. John Anderdon, apparently in good health, died suddenly in 1872 and the family suffered the loss of their second son. Although John Anderdon of Henlade had married there were no children.

So once again Henlade House was in need of an owner. Henry Murray, first son of FHM, grandson of John Lavicount Anderdon and nephew to John Anderdon of Henlade, was next in line. He was now aged about 24 years, took the name Murray-Anderdon and became the master of the Henlade Estate. This was a lucky moment for Henry. Family letters expressed concern over Henry's progress and prospects: 'Henry [up at Oxford] has been plucked again and I can't find that he did well in anything. Francis evidently suffers although he expresses little – do not write to Henry. I do so. I hope that by God's gracious will this may prove a turning point in his character – call out his religious sense of what he owes to so excellent a father.' This was in a letter from John Anderdon to Anne, written in June. It was in October of that year that the death occurred of John Anderdon of Henlade and Henry's future was assured.

In fact, 'Henlade and all its temptations' (John Anderdon's words) were to prove the perfect setting for Henry: he possessed a sociable personality and maintained, with his wife, a *ménage* of renowned hospitality. His particular achievement was to put the Somerset County Cricket Club on its feet and assume the office of President. Henry, who married twice but had no issue, died in 1922. Yet again Henlade did not pass from father to son.

* * *

From 1850 the Anderdon family had more or less based themselves in Chislehurst allowing for John Anderdon's necessary absences up in London and, at one time, their home in Chislehurst was at the bottom of Church Row. John Anderdon was a writer of some note and his biography of Bishop Ken, published in 1851, is a standard work. He was an enthusiastic fisherman and inspired by a walking tour through Derbyshire he compiled an attractive book, *The River Dove with some quiet thoughts on the Practice of Angling* – rather in the style of *The Compleat Angler* by Izaak Walton. He cared anxiously for his family, urging his daughters home if he thought they had stayed away too long either because he missed them or because he was worried that they were outstaying their welcome. He was distressed that Maria and Anne had not married.

He enjoyed the 'social circle round Chislehurst Common . . . with the dear church and Pastor the centre of it all' and odd sentences in his letters give glimpses of Chislehurst life at that time. 'We have just presented old Glide[9] with a new red flannel night cap to keep the t-t-tips of his ears-s-s warm.' He was a supporter of the village amateur dramatics – in fact some of the family took parts: 'John took on at half an hour's notice . . . his acting is something to speak of . . . Helen played her part very well, quite the fair lady . . . encored in one inimitable scene . . . the play is to be repeated at Mrs Wollaston's by special request.' He goes on to describe the audience: 'We had 30 or 40 of the middle class including the schoolmaster and mistresses. Mr Dumbleton [the curate] laughed out most amiable, indeed no-one could resist.'

Another letter speaks of his efforts with the village men: 'The night school rather thrives. I think I am getting my rough chaps into a little order and a sense of something rather better than at first'. When visiting his sick father he writes home with instructions to give something to a poor family he has adopted: '. . . they are placed under my care and woe be to me if I fare sumptuously and they hunger'.

A few weeks before he died in 1874, he wrote to his early business partner, Frederick, describing the efficient nursing he was receiving from the hands of his daughter Maria. He conjured up a picture of a loving family surrounding him with every attention. Getting to bed was a long drawn out affair requiring much assistance, for example in climbing the stairs, but the night-time procedure always included the reading aloud of a good book by Maria.

By unfortunate coincidence, his funeral took place on the very day that Chislehurst enjoyed the excitement of all the comings and goings at Camden Place for the coming of age[10] of the Prince Imperial, son of the late Emperor Napoleon III.

The philanthropic attitude of the family can be seen in the enduring innovations of the daughters. Their financial position improved in time as small inheritances came their way and the first fruit of their altruism was the Orphanage.

> We bought a plot of parish ground
> to make an Orphanage home for boys;
> with twenty we began
> but applications by the score
> incessantly upon us pour;
> we soon enlarge again.

Maria seems to have been the spirit behind the curriculum and the homeliness of the institution – she was 'like a mother to her large family'.

Another project was the group of residences known as the Manning and Anderdon Almshouses, founded in 1881: 'Inmates must be poor, more or less 12 years resident in Chislehurst and of good moral and religious character.'

Helen, the youngest of the Anderdon daughters, comes across as of an entirely different generation for she craved a career in teaching and went to college in London – although there is no mention of her actually doing a teaching job. At a friend's wedding she met and afterwards married Thomas Salt,[11] later Sir Thomas and sometime Member of Parliament for Stafford. It was through her marriage only that the Anderdon line continued.

After her husband's death Anna Maria Anderdon went to live in accommodation at the Orphanage and she was finally buried next to her husband on the north side of St Nicholas' churchyard. Anne Anderdon died in 1892 and Maria in 1904: 'As long as she [Maria] was able her day began with attendance at the Holy Communion – and she came in all weathers, even when she could only get to church with assistance – while she was seldom absent from the Daily Offices.'[12]

This brief description hardly does them justice but in their close and loving family life, and in their piety, the Anderdons are examples of the particular sort of Victorian family who ensured that villages like Chislehurst flourished: paternalistic they may have been, but then, this was the nineteenth century.

* * *

A description of the Anderdon family would not be complete without following up the subsequent life of Henry Murray-Anderdon.

The Anderdons and the Mannings were connected by both Harrow School and a passion for cricket. In the 1820s the boys of Harrow School, who organised their own sport, were so keen to improve their skills that they hired, at their own expense, a cricket coach; none other than John Lavicount Anderdon. There was a remarkable match in 1825 when the Harrow Eleven contained Henry Manning, Richard Trench and Charles Wordsworth: 'a unique trinity of a future cardinal, an archbishop and a bishop'.[13]

by permission of Somerset County Cricket Club Museum

H. E. Murray-Anderdon

Henry Edward Murray, strangely, was not an old Harrovian but was equally keen on cricket and featured in many Chislehurst matches, even after he had taken over his Somerset property in 1872. It was not until 1885, when he became Secretary, that he came to the forefront of Somerset County cricket. The club had suffered many match defeats, morale was low and support was dwindling. The advent of the stylish Henry galvanised the situation: 'Inheriting a factional and practically bankrupt club he managed to revive finances, buy a lovely ground and build a team strong enough to enter the County Championship in 1891'.[14]

Henry's 'style' seems to have been a powerful force in the building up of the club: 'He had a commanding aristocratic manner. His orders were incisive. He arrived at the ground in a chauffeur-driven Daimler in later years . . . cricket, along with fishing, was his passion . . . He played occasionally for the Club but very much down the order and with minimal success but he was a fine administrator and his job was to shake the place up'.[15]

He sported a fine dark beard of which he was proud: this had been grown originally because he had difficulty in tying his bow or cravat after one arm was badly and permanently injured. The accident had occurred, incongruously, when he had been knocked down by a steam roller outside his front gate.

After becoming involved he soon realised that Somerset needed better players. It was his idea that local clergy should be phased out and young talent brought in from the Universities of Oxford and Cambridge. 'No-one would say that Somerset was a team without brains.'[16]

Henry stood down from the Secretary's job in 1910 after twenty five years and served as President from 1915 until his death in 1922. As the County Gazette commented: 'He was one of a handful of giants in the story of Somerset's cricket'.

He was succeeded at Henlade by a son of Helen (daughter of John Lavicount Anderdon) and Sir Thomas Salt. Herbert Edward Salt assumed the name Anderdon by Deed Poll in 1923.

---

1 The Manning family has Chislehurst connections: in Webb's *History of Chislehurst* can be seen the descent of the families of Manning and Anderdon from Hugh Manning of Cray in the time of Henry VII.

2 E.S. Purcell, *Life of Cardinal Manning.*

3 Robert Gray, *Cardinal Manning.*

4 Henry Edward Manning was the uncle of Fanny Anderdon. One wonders whether Fanny and Francis named their first son after him. We know from Webb's *History of Chislehurst* that Manning played cricket in Chislehurst in 1823 and that he frequently visited the Anderdon family when they lived in Chislehurst.

5 He was made Archdeacon of Chichester at the age of 33 while holding the living of Lavington in Sussex.

6 The remaining son, Samuel, became Bishop of Oxford, and then Winchester. He was famous for the Darwin debate with Huxley.

7 Owen Chadwick, *The Victorian Church.*

8 Cardinal Manning's funeral in 1892 was an occasion of overwhelming emotion for the public: the procession wound for four miles through the streets of London where the pavements were thronged with mourners who crammed every window and doorstep. However, it was some years before Manning was treated to a kind biography. Edmund Purcell's immediate biography, based largely on purloined material, was sensational in approach making much of Manning's ambitious nature rather than his prominence in social work and his successful mediation in the 1889 London Dock Strike. Lytton Strachey's essay in *Eminent Victorians,* influenced by Purcell's book, was not a generous piece of work.

9 The Glide family were bellringers and William Glide was Parish Beadle.

10 'The railway station was gaily decorated and flew the Tricoleur of France, whilst in the waiting room an inscription, wreathed in laurels and violets read "Vive le Prince Imperial". An address was presented on behalf of the inhabitants.' Tom Bushell, *Imperial Chislehurst.*

11 It was he who designed the orphanage house, described in *The History of Chislehurst* as 'a pretty building of brick and timber, forming with the institution a picturesque group . . .'

12 From her privately printed obituary.

13 Christopher Tyerman, *A History of Harrow School.*

14 Peter Roebuck, *From Sammy to Jimmy.* (Sammy Woods and Jimmy Cook – two Somerset players.)

15 David Foot, *Sunshine, Sixes and Cider.*

16 David Foot, *op.cit.*

Chapter 9

Societas Sanctae Crucis
(part one)
Friendship with Charles Fuge Lowder

. . . a most excellent sermon yesterday from Newman . . . none could rejoice more than the preacher himself at the increased regard for ecclesiastical architecture, music, the ornamenting of our churches etc., but still it must be recollected that these require to be accompanied by personal holiness and that even the spirit of devotion might become little better than a luxurious pleasure, unless we maintain a spirit of self denial in it, to remind us that we are not to make everything so much a gratification to ourselves, as a sacrifice to God.

A letter[1] *from* CHARLES LOWDER *to his parents*
from Exeter College, Oxford.

Three chapters on Charles Fuge Lowder might at first appear to detract attention from the subject of this book but in fact the two lives were so intertwined that it is necessary to explain why Lowder is so important. He was buried, at his own request, in St Nicholas' Churchyard and the Church of England celebrates his life each year on the 9th September.

Lowder was born in the same year as FHM and although their educational routes were not parallel they each experienced the impact of the Oxford Movement when at Oxford and came away committed to the ideal of conducting their ministries along Tractarian lines. It could be that they did not actually meet until 1855, that is, at the founding of the organisation named *Societas Sanctae Crucis*. Their working lives were set in vastly differing circumstances but there was mutual trust and the certainty of mutual support. However, a taste they shared was for travelling abroad and when FHM was away Lowder took over some of the duties in Chislehurst – but not in their entirety as there were always one or two curates[2] in the parish.

Lowder claims a place, not only in a history based on Chislehurst but also in the larger history of the Church of England, for he was a major figure both in the violently controversial development of ritualistic services and also in the rescue of the thousands of souls beached up helplessly in overcrowded city slums: Owen Chadwick describes him as 'one of the great slum priests of the century'.[3]

To introduce him it is necessary to go back to his curacy at St Barnabas' Church, Pimlico, and to re-state the problem of simmering anti-Roman Catholic hostility. This embraced also a hostility to any hints of Catholicism in the Established Church of England and it has already featured on one occasion in Chislehurst when the cross on Fanny Murray's grave was vandalised in 1850, the year of the so called act of Papal

by permission of Rev. Canon Michael Shields SSC

Charles Fuge Lowder

Aggression. Vestments, lighted candles, intoning of services etc., were appearing at this time but the innovations, perceived to be 'Roman', met obstruction from every quarter. Opposition came from both lay people and Bishops. The power of the latter to block advancement of clergy and close churches caused most distress: after all, clergy had at Ordination promised 'reverently to obey' their Bishops 'following with a glad mind and will their godly admonitions'.

As early as 1851, St Barnabas', Pimlico, whose status was that of a chapel-of-ease to St Paul's, Knightsbridge, had gained a reputation for Popery amongst those who were on the look-out for such an 'aberration'. *The Ecclesiologist* called it 'the most complete . . . and most sumptuous church which had been dedicated since the [Catholic] revival'. At the daily Communion Service the clergy, vested in surplice, hood and controversial stole, celebrated at a stone altar. The church had been dedicated in 1850 and it is therefore not surprising that Low Churchmen and also the ever-willing 'mob' were ready to target St Barnabas', popular though it was with the few who attended.

In 1854 the continued interruption of services and the rowdy election of Churchwardens gave an excuse to the choirboys to deal with the matter in their own way. It was through his young nephew who, in the school holidays, had befriended the choirboys that Lowder learned of the intention to use stones to pelt the unfortunate sandwich-man who was drumming up support for a hostile churchwarden candidate. Lowder gave them sixpence to purchase rotten eggs as missiles, instead of stones. This act of 'kindness' earned Lowder a six-week suspension of his licence. On the face of it, Bishop Blomfield of London was displeased but in fact, privately, the Bishop was rather amused and referred to the event as Mr Lowder's 'ovation'.

So, for a period of six weeks, he was forced to leave behind his work in the slums of Pimlico: this included parochial visiting, day and night schools, charitable institutions and a house of refuge for prostitutes. With painful economy he travelled to a school near Rouen under the direction of a M. Labbé who gave him to read *Vie de Saint Vincent de Paul* during the course of his stay. Reading the book revealed to Lowder the many similarities between the religious condition of the France of the late sixteenth century and the England of the middle of the nineteenth century and he determined, when he returned, to found a society in England to correspond with St Vincent's *Prêtres de la Congrégation de la Mission.*

* * *

On 28th February 1855 Lowder and five other clergy held the inaugural meeting of the Society of the Holy Cross, usually referred to by the initials of its Latin name SSC – *Societas Sanctae Crucis*. The very name was challenging: not only was it in Latin but also it celebrated the Cross – at that time an inflammatory symbol of Popery. The establishment of a society thus named made a clear statement – that its members held dear the unbroken inheritance of the true Catholic Church. In 1876, when the SSC was celebrating its 21st year, the Master[4] looked back on the reasons for the Society's formation: it sprang out of 'the necessity of meeting the belief and disbelief of the day and of meeting the increasing opposition to Catholic life'. This was to be achieved by a combined action, on however small a scale, of greater personal mortification, more entire corporate unity and a supreme sense of Brotherhood.

This first meeting[5] was held at the House of Charity, Rose St, Soho: the six clergy were vested in surplice and stole. '[They] said the Office of the Society together in Latin at 3pm after which they severally made the Promise of Secrecy, the Profession of Faith and the Promise of Mutual Help. The Pax having been exchanged the brethren adjourned to the Council Room.'

The Promise of Secrecy bound the member 'never knowingly to disclose any of the Rules, Plans or Proceedings of the SSC' unless by special command of the same society and 'whether I be in or out of the aforesaid society.'

The Promise of Mutual Aid concluded: 'Moreover, I will not speak evil, even upon great provocation of any member of this society to anyone, except the Master and Vicars of the same.'

The Pax consisted of a ceremony in which the cross was passed round to all present, each kissing it and passing it on. Finally, the Master would say 'Brethren, go in the Peace of our Lord Jesus Christ.'

On 14th September, the Feast of the Holy Cross, the Minute Book records: 'A conference was held with the Rev. G.C. White[6] and the Rev. F.H. Murray about the object of the Society . . . Rev. White and Rev. Murray were elected conditionally in their so pressing a desire to become members of the Society'.

These early meetings were only sparsely attended, often only three or four were present. On the 13th October FHM made the required promise and was admitted to the SSC. At the meeting on 6th November he was already absorbed sufficiently to be asked, with Br White (George Cosby White) and with one of the founder members, to prepare the 'Voluntary Rule' for the single and married brethren.

From the start it was Lowder's intention that the SSC should function with the structure of a closed order: an important aim was 'the cultivation of personal holiness'. At the beginning, indeed throughout the first twenty years at least, the refinement of the wording of the 'Rules' was a regular part of the business. The following summary of the system comes from L.E. Ellsworth's *Charles Lowder and the Ritualist Movement*, the classic life of Lowder.

'. . . the SSC first drafted a set of rules to apply to all members, enforcing daily prayer for the Church and Society, mutual aid and encouragement, attendance at SSC synods in May and monthly chapters when possible, contributions to the society's treasury, and so on; and then a trio of voluntary rules for life – the White, Red and Green Rules – to be taken according to the situation and inclination of individual members. The White Rule was a formidable guide to holiness intended for such members as chose to be celibate, enjoining daily Holy Communion, extensive prayer, frequent self-examination, daily study and meditation, control of the senses, restraint in speech and recreation, abstinence and fasting.'[7]

The Red Rule, not much less demanding than the White Rule, was for married and single men and the Green Rule became the ordinary rule of the Society, binding upon all brethren. At one time there was a thought that Sisters of Mercy and ordinands should be enrolled at the basic level but the decision was rescinded: the secrecy element had to be guarded carefully, so great was the suspicion in the minds of the general public of emerging ritualism. Lowder wished to avoid the violence already experienced in Pimlico.

* * *

Two important developments occurred at the beginning of 1856, the first being the introduction of Retreats. Lowder's vision included the revival of Retreats for the sustaining of the spiritual life of the clergy and indeed St Vincent de Paul had been a strong advocate of the practice. When the SSC sought a venue for the Church of England's first Retreat since pre-Reformation times FHM volunteered his Rectory in Chislehurst. So, for a week during February in 1856, the people of Chislehurst would have been witness to clerical comings and goings between the Rectory and the Church. This would become familiar as the years went by.[8] At this first Retreat at Chislehurst, according to J. Embry's history of the SSC, 'there was no silence and no meditation. But there was held a spiritual Conference after Nones, special subjects were chosen for prayer and intercession at Mass,[9] and all the Day Office was said.' The Bishop of Brechin described the Retreat movement's beginnings at Chislehurst thus: 'The picturesque old Rectory at Chislehurst has the honour of inaugurating a species of devotion which, whether under the name of Retreats or Quiet Days, has become so universally prevalent since as to be a thing of annual or more frequent occurrence, not only in towns but often in remote villages.'

The first Ignatian[10] style retreat, FHM acting as bursar, was led by SSC member R.M. Benson at Cuddesdon near Oxford, where there is now a Theological College.

R.M. Benson was to be the founder of the Cowley Fathers, Oxford: in a letter to his mother on his satisfaction at the success of the retreat he said: 'We had a nice little company, eleven and sometimes twelve. One or two of them were of such advanced holiness that it made one quite ashamed to sit as a teacher.'

* * *

The second development came as a result of Lowder's expressed desire to establish a home mission among the poor. SSC members were asked in January whether they knew of a parish which would welcome such a move. FHM responded by talking about the matter in Chislehurst with one of his churchwardens, Thomas Charrington, owner of a big business in Shadwell in the Docks area of East London. This conversation soon led to an offer by the Rev. Bryan King, Rector of St George's-in-the-East: he agreed that on Mondays, Wednesdays and Fridays evening services should be conducted in a parish schoolroom by two priests, one at least being an SSC member.

King did indeed need help with his 30,000 parishioners: not only was he being persecuted, as were the clergy at St Barnabas', Pimlico, but the vast majority of his parishioners were utterly ignorant of the Gospel, in fact so distant from religion as to be unaware of the problems at the church. The mission started in a truly godless part of London – the like of which, it must be pointed out, could be found over and over again in the metropolis. According to J. Embry,[11] FHM and Cosby White were the first two SSC members to take a mission meeting after the Ash Wednesday opening by Lowder but in the well-ordered, hierarchical society of Chislehurst FHM and Cosby White had little experience of the deprived and corrupted society that existed in a dockland area. However, it was not long before the missioners realised that those who attended the meetings were solely the faithful few who were already worshipping at St George's-in-the-East: the missioners were not attracting the masses who had never set foot in the church.

A slum is, by definition, squalid and urban: the word carries with it images of filth and disease, poverty and degradation, neglect, decay, exploitation, crime. All these were to be found near the riverside in the overcrowded parish of St George's and it was amid these horrors that the Mission needed to operate. Therefore, after about a fortnight, the mission moved further into the dockside area, to miserable premises in Lower Well Alley, Wapping; by April 1856 the Mission had become a permanent fixture with Lowder, now aged 36, at its head. The Mission finally settled in two centres; one in Wellclose Square and one in Calvert Street where a church of corrugated iron was erected.

Initially, problems came from the Irish, formerly encouraged there in large numbers for the business of digging out the docks. The Church of England at the time of the Mission fell broadly into two camps, the Protestant Evangelicals, called Low Church, and the newly developing Anglo-Catholics whom I have chosen, mostly, to call Tractarians.[12] The secession of so many of the early Tractarians to the Church of Rome had not helped the Anglo-Catholic cause and the presence of Lowder and his team of clergy was loathsome to the Roman Catholic Irish labourers – far more antagonising than any Low Church element in their midst. They formed disorderly gangs for the purpose of disrupting preaching by noisy uproar and violence.

But it was not only rude interruptions that made the preaching ineffective. Unfortunately, Lowder and his clergy helpers had no idea of how to approach the type of people they had in front of them: the phrase 'horses for courses' springs to mind. Only a few years earlier William Booth, later 'General Booth' of The Salvation Army, had been only a short distance away working as a pawnbroker's assistant: 'The years in the East End of London amongst the slums of the Mile End Road and the stews of Limehouse had introduced him to the hard reality of pawnbroking as it affected the very poor – the sacrifice of the last remaining possessions for the price of a bottle of gin.'[13] With this experience, William Booth was equipped to make a much more direct and aggressive appeal to the poor, unhindered by too much learning. In contrast, according to a Rev. Rowley, one of the Wapping missioners, Lowder's sermons 'were frequently more suitable for the dwellers in the cloister than for the inhabitants of one of the most degraded parts of London'.[14]

In these early days, St George's Mission, as it was known, seemed a hopeless cause and indeed, some of the missioners dropped away. Lowder, austere in looks and austere in character, was a hard leader to follow and demanded much of his colleagues, but as is so often the case if you cannot fault your master you learn to emulate and admire him.

Self discipline was essential for the Mission clergy who had, unflinching, to enter premises whose sordidness beggared belief and whose occupants suffered unspeakably wretched lives. Madge Darby quotes from one of the clergy who describes a typical family: 'Having struggled up the narrow rickety stairs, and passed lower regions peopled with men, women and children, who open their doors in curiosity to gaze at us and thus reveal the hideous misery within, we come to a garret where a poor woman lies dying on the floor, huddled into a corner on a bag of straw, covered over for the sake of warmth with all the rags which constitute the property of the place. One is half stifled with the intolerable smell. At a glance we take in the awful poverty, for literally there is not a stick of furniture save the crazy looking table and one broken chair. The children – well, I have seen them quite naked like savages. Perhaps even in the depth of winter no fire in the grate. Of the horrors of vermin one cannot speak. We are told, and we could have guessed it from their faces, that they had not food that day.'

Clearly, social conditions like these needed a large army of helpers to bring about any kind of amelioration. In 1854 Rev. John Mason Neale, a co-founder of the Cambridge Camden Society and later to be known for his prolific hymn-writing,[15] had founded with his sister Elizabeth the Anglican Sisterhood of St Margaret in East Grinstead. In 1857 Lowder agreed that a sisterhood should be established in Wapping and he and Mother Elizabeth formed the Community of the Holy Cross. (Lowder, incidentally, was the first Anglican priest to be known as 'Father': this appellation was first used around 1866.) The Sisterhood provided a refuge for girls who desired to give up prostitution but such was the attraction of the protection and improved living conditions that girls would resort to pretence in order to gain admission. At a later date the refuge in Wapping became just a stepping stone as it seemed wiser to take the girls out of the area in order to start new lives. Additionally, the members of the order assisted with practical involvement in the lives of the poor, providing clothing and bedding for the needy and, most importantly, set up schools for the children.

* * *

It was at this time that the whole issue of Ritualism came to a head although the end of strife was still a long way off. It was certainly not one of the ideals of the original Oxford Movement to develop a ritualistic Church patterned on Rome. However, there was already provision for daily service, private confession and splendid ornaments if the ornaments rubric of the Book of Common Prayer were interpreted sympathetically. Pusey and Newman did not care, at that time, to go along the ritualistic path for fear of losing the greater impact of the religious revolution resulting from the Oxford Movement: in any case, they thought these extras were unnecessary. But many, including Lowder, saw ceremonial, splendid vestments and ornate interiors as aids to the spiritual life. Lowder in particular knew that he was making religion attractive to the dockland worshippers at his church: their daily circumstances were drab and uninspiring but to enter a church with gold, candles, singing and dramatic ceremony provided a glimpse of heaven.

Ritualism was causing uproar throughout the country but St George's-in-the-East and Lowder's Mission were singled out as a focus. At St George's itself, for a variety of reasons, the attacks were particularly virulent: at one stage in 1859 Bishop Tait of London had to close the church for a few weeks. The scenes are described in Owen Chadwick, *The Victorian Church*: '. . . Sunday afternoons at St George's were the zoo and horror and coconut shy of London. The best days witnessed pew doors banging or feet scraping or hissing or coughing or syncopated responses. The worst days witnessed gleeful rows of boys shooting with peas from the gallery, fireworks, flaming speeches from tub-orators during service, bleating as of goats, spitting on choirboys, a pair of hounds howling gin-silly round the nave, cushions hurled at the altar, orange peel and butter, kicking or hustling of clergy. One of the altar carpets was crammed into a stove and pew no.16 in the south aisle was used as a privy. Lowder once had to flee from the crowd . . . In June 1860 seventy three policemen were stationed at St George's Church every Sunday. Bryan King consented to take a prolonged holiday and left early in the morning to escape the brass band which opponents hired to escort him to the station.'

It could be argued that Bryan King probably showed too fanatical a determination by continuing with his ritualistic services but, in a strange way, the opposition he provoked gave strength to clergy: to drop the ritualism after the St George's fiasco was to be cowardly. Lowder's Mission Church had not suffered as much as St George's itself because, not being an official Parish Church, it was possible to allow entry by ticket only. However, it was not unscathed: 'The purveyors of vice, whose trade Lowder had attacked took advantage of the situation to stir up the riots and paid hooligans to attack the mission. The Rev. Mackonochie was assaulted by the mob and had to be rescued by the police. Lowder's life was in danger as the rioters threatened to throw him over the bridge into the docks: but he faced the infuriated mob with dauntless courage.'[16]

The lasting effect of the rioting was to the advantage of the mission. Respect for Lowder's courage brought an increased congregation and soon the Iron Church, designed for only two hundred, could not hold all of those who clamoured to attend services.

* * *

Throughout this time Lowder and Bryan King received support from the members of the SSC: within the Society it was 'business as usual'. Monthly meetings continued as before but, after the violence, it was more necessary than ever to maintain the confidentiality of proceedings. New members came forward including a steady stream of Chislehurst curates and also FHM's brother, Frederick Murray of Stone, near Dartford. Donations or letters of sympathy were sent to help clergy who were suffering for their innovations.[17] Pamphlets were issued on a variety of topics, for example, a *Manual of Devotions for the Poor*: the problem of Devotions for those who could not read was an urgent matter. The question of evening celebrations of Holy Communion was addressed – the practice was described as an 'evil' and five thousand copies of a tract against Evening Celebrations were distributed. Something as controversial as the taking of Communion by children who had not yet been confirmed was looked on with favour and, in individual churches, developments such as the Parish Magazine[18] and the provision of a table for pamphlets at the church door were the work of SSC members.

However, the SSC could not be accused of a narrow, conservative belief in its own approach. Agreed, they high-mindedly wished 'to dig the pit for the cross' in London but were more than willing to admit the success of the 'strange method' of the American evangelists, Sankey and Moody, who could, with hindsight, be said to have pioneered the Billy Graham style: '. . . the Holy Spirit did sometimes work in other channels external to the church, and that unCatholic England might, in the first instance, be touched by unCatholic means . . .' (This was in the 1870s.)

Lowder was concerned about the shortage of candidates for Holy Orders, especially from the 'poorer classes' and wished to see training available to such men as were keen to be missionaries. In a statement that reflected the class-ridden ethos of the time 'Br Chambers disagreed and dwelt on the tendency of men so trained to abandon the missionary life for the sake of social advancement'. By now, 1861-2, the SSC had provincial Chapters and a report was sent from Oxford on a scheme for the erection of a private hall in Oxford to enable poor scholars to come up to the University. Already there was a 'college' of students attached to St Thomas's Church 'where men might have this education at Oxford for £50 a year' and stay up for the whole year helping at a Parish Church.

The Minute Books record FHM's regular attendance at the monthly meetings of the SSC, his frequent contributions to discussion and the writing of papers for synod:

he was almost perpetually a holder of the office of Vicar until his resignation[19] in 1877.

SSC members continued with their rigid personal régime. The Red Rule specified, for example, that 'members should avoid all theatres, balls, cards and any public amusements except music, in which there was nothing immoral.' They were 'to restrain curiosity' and to limit their 'reading about sin (as in trials in newspapers) except as a duty'. They were 'never to repeat evil, or speak disparagingly of anyone except as a distinct duty or rather endeavour to make an excuse for anyone who may be evil spoken of, or speak some good of them or, if none be known, be silent or turn the conversation. Do not interrupt others in conversation but allow yourself to be interrupted and often keep silence as a mode of self-discipline and collectedness. Avoid frivolous and unedifying conversation, especially in female company. Finally, never quote Holy Scriptures except for religious ends.'

* * *

The thread that ran through the SSC reports was the headway of the mission in Wapping. Although progress was apparent the question of funding was serious: the clergy team and their helpers were as poor as their people. Initially, they had had a cottage at Chislehurst as an escape from the foetid[20] air of the East End but funds could not be found to maintain this idea. At one time the suggestion was that they should give up their clergy house in Wapping and make do in the vestry of the church. They ate frugally and one visitor commented that portions were so small that there was little room for self denial.

Lowder's sister had come to live in Chislehurst and she made pleas for St George's Mission in the Parish Magazine. FHM and his curates gave constant support, particularly to Lowder who was given a room at the Rectory for recuperation. Lowder loved Chislehurst and, when he was there, played a part in the running of the parish: the school log book, for example, records his frequent trips across the common to give lessons to the children.

The first part of Charles Lowder's story ends with the triumph of the building and consecration of the new church of St Peter's, London Docks.[21] Having outgrown the beloved old Iron Church, the replacement was dedicated, unfinished because of lack of funds, in June 1866 by Bishop Tait of London. Tait's presence was a particular joy to Lowder for the Bishop had been wary of, if not hostile to, the style that Lowder was promoting. On this great occasion the streets were decked with flags and schoolchildren lined the route.

Lowder wrote afterwards: 'It was a day ever to be remembered in the history of the Mission, whether for the fulfilment of long-indulged anticipations in the sight of a duly consecrated church, the beauty and solemn character of St Peter's, the full attendance of clergy and friends, or, above all, for the hearty sympathy of the Bishop in the work of the Mission.'

---

1 Quoted by L.E. Ellsworth, *Charles Lowder and the Ritualist Movement.*

2 At the beginning of 1858 FHM suffered a bout of illness and was not helped by the presence of an

unsatisfactory curate. According to John L. Anderdon only the presence in Chislehurst of Lowder could give him the peace of mind to benefit from a recuperative holiday.

3 Owen Chadwick, *The Victorian Church.*

4 All members referred to themselves as Brethren and there was a hierarchy of a Master and four Vicars, corresponding with the four arms of the Cross.

5 Details of meetings have been taken from the SSC minute books which were at one time held at the Centre for Kentish Studies, Maidstone.

6 Rev. George Cosby White, FHM's Curate: mentioned earlier in connection with *A&M.*

7 Lowder and two others undertook the White Rule in December 1855.

8 FHM was by now re-married and this must surely be an indication of the support he received from Mary.

9 'Mass' was not a word that FHM liked to use. (SSC Minutes 1878.)

10 The Jesuits were the first religious order to include Retreats in their rule and the practice harks back to Jesus' 40 days in the wilderness. An Ignatian retreat is conducted in silence and occupied with meditation and religious exercises.

11 J. Embry, *The Catholic Movement and SSC.*

12 'High Church' would not be quite the correct description. High Church had existed for a long time but was not necessarily Catholic. In fact, High Church and Low Church were, to a certain extent, political labels: High = Tory, Low = Whig.

13 Roy Hattersley, *Blood and Fire – William and Catherine Booth and Their Salvation Army.*

14 Madge Darby, *The first Hundred Years at St Peter's, London Docks.*

15 More than sixty of his hymns appeared in *A&M.*

16 Madge Darby, *op. cit.*

17 From the SSC minutes of 3rd May, 1859: 'Br Murray proposed that £5 should be devoted to the Poole Defence Fund.' Alfred Poole, a founder member of the SSC and curate at St Barnabas' had had his licence withdrawn by the Bishop of London on the matter of confession, a topic guaranteed to inflame and to become later the cause of the near-downfall of the SSC.

18 The credit for the introduction of Parish Magazines goes to SSC member W.J.E. Bennett of Frome in Somerset. Bennett was a controversial figure in the context of Ritualism : he was the first incumbent of St Barnabas', Pimlico. His publication, from 1854 until 1862, *The Old Church Porch*, was not the locally written magazine that we now know but it was distributed in parishes in the same way and developed a local slant. Chislehurst's first magazine came out in 1867.

19 The matter of his resignation will be considered in Chapter 14.

20 Not only was the air bad because of all the riverside industries and the unhygienic conditions in people's houses but also because this was the era of The Great Stink when all London's river neighbourhood was unbearable. It got so bad that Parliament was considering a move to a more salubrious place. The problem was sewage and was only solved by the great works of Sir Joseph Bazalgette.

21 Although it suffered some war damage this church is still an active parish church with a strong Anglo-Catholic tradition. The neighbourhood, needless to say, has been magnificently 'upgraded'.

Chapter 10

Criticism at St Nicholas'

I have reason to believe that there are many of the parishioners and heads of families who also disapprove of the proceedings of the Rector and object to the doctrines held by him, that [sic] who, for various reasons still attend the church.

A letter from LORD SYDNEY
to ARCHBISHOP LONGLEY of CANTERBURY.

Just as the East End storm against ritualism began to subside,[1] quietened in that particular spot by the time of the foundation of St Peter's, London Docks, a mild squall blew up over Chislehurst. It was so discreet that it is unlikely that more than a handful of people in Chislehurst knew of it. The instigator of the trouble was John Robert Townshend, Lord Sydney.

Viewed from this distance Lord Sydney is not a clearly defined character and, in the absence of much information to the contrary, it is only too easy to think ill of him.

Lord Sydney's family, the Townshends, were every bit as illustrious as the Murrays and similarly peppered with characters who hovered near the throne, fought battles or fell in and out of favour politically. There was one moment when a Murray may well have ridden alongside a Townshend for each was in the company of the Duke of Cumberland at the Battle of Culloden.

However, in general, the facts are that the Murrays were Tories and the Townshends were Whigs: the Murrays went to Harrow and Oxford and the Townshends went to Eton and Cambridge. As for churchmanship, the Murrays were High Church and the Townshends were Low Church.

The Townshend family originated in Norfolk, Rainham Hall being the family seat, and there is one ancestor whom everyone knows about. After a fall from political favour in 1730, John Robert's great, great grandfather Charles Townshend, a volatile character of the first order, retired to his Norfolk estate in order to spend more time with his family(!) and to make agricultural improvements on his estate. At Rainham he carried out agricultural experiments which earned him the nickname 'Turnip Townshend' and, according to Alexander Pope, turnips and their uses were 'the favourite subject of Townshend's conversation'.[2]

It was Turnip Townshend's son, Thomas, who founded a branch of the family in Chislehurst. He married the sixteen year old Albinia,[3] daughter and heiress of Col. John Selwyn[4] of Gloucestershire who had, by a family arrangement, purchased the Lordship of the Manors of Chislehurst and Scadbury. Selwyn then settled Scadbury on his son-in-law. Thomas demolished the old moated house, intending to rebuild it, but sadly, after bearing five children, Albinia died in 1739 at the age of 24, leaving her husband too grief-stricken to proceed with the new house. After Selwyn's death in

Bust of John Robert Townshend 1st Earl Sydney of Scadbury. Sculptor: Sir S.J.E. Boehm

1751, Thomas Townshend purchased Frognal, but retained ownership of the Scadbury estate. This is why the Townshend family came to be at Frognal and yet remain in 'ownership' of the Scadbury Chapel, in the north-east corner of St Nicholas' Church.

The eldest son of Albinia and Thomas, also Thomas, was created the first Viscount Sydney in 1789 after having been relieved of his post as Secretary of State under William Pitt. However, shortly before this he had, unwittingly, made a name for himself, the significance of which would long outlive the placatory title of Viscount. In the hope that the convicts shipped to New South Wales, Australia, would form the nucleus of a colony a little town was founded in Port Jackson: this was named Sydney as a tribute to the Secretary of State. He died in Chislehurst in 1800.

The second Viscount Sydney, John Thomas Townshend, held office as under-Secretary of State under his father, as a Lord of the Admiralty and finally as a Lord of the Treasury but gave up his political career on succeeding to his father's title. It was then that he entered into the personal service of the sovereign as Lord of the Bedchamber to George III from 1800-1810 and it was in similar capacities that his son, John Robert Townshend, spent his life.

The third Viscount, commonly known as Lord Sydney in Chislehurst, was Lord of the Bedchamber to William IV, Lord in Waiting to Queen Victoria, Lord Chamberlain of the Household in Gladstone's first administration and Lord Steward of the Household in Gladstone's second and third administrations. These are only a few of the offices he held. In 1874, 'at the special desire of the Queen, in recognition of his valuable services to Her Majesty' he was awarded the title of Earl Sydney of Scadbury. Indeed, there seems to have been some affection on the part of the Queen for her loyal courtier and certainly on one occasion she paid a visit to Frognal. This was in April 1872. It is recorded that when Queen Elizabeth I had paid a visit to nearby Scadbury she had planted some fig trees which had come from Marseilles.[5] These very trees were pointed out to Queen Victoria by Lord Sydney.

Lord Sydney had the dubious distinction of being the subject of one of the earliest caricatures in the periodical *Vanity Fair* when it came out in 1869. His fly-away hair, rather like Denis Healey's eyebrows, lent itself to exaggeration and his pose would best be described as truculent.

The accompanying 'witty' paragraphs were not very funny – rather scathing in fact. The general gist was that Lord Sydney, an eminent Liberal, could hardly exercise powers of statesmanship in his role as Lord Chamberlain but he was nevertheless assuming an enormously important role in the regulation of the current laws of etiquette. The satirist wondered at his audacity in refusing invitations to Royal Balls (for reasons that could only be guessed at) and also in 'recommending increased drapery to theatrical managers'. This last is a reference to a letter he sent to all metropolitan theatre managers complaining of the impropriety of costume of the ladies in Pantomimes, Burlesques etc. ' . . . many who have hitherto frequented the theatres now profess themselves unwilling to permit the ladies of their families to sanction by their presence such questionable exhibitions'. The Lord Chamberlain appealed to theatre managers to assist in abating the evil which threatened to become a public scandal.

* * *

It was in February 1867 that Lord Sydney's indignation about the Rector of Chislehurst caused him to write to the Archbishop of Canterbury. By now there were daily public services in St Nicholas' Church, and an early celebration of Holy Communion on each Sunday. Both greater and lesser festivals were observed and in Holy Week there were daily services. Although FHM could be described as an advanced Tractarian this provision was modest compared with that in some places: there were still only minimal vestments worn at Holy Communion (this continued until 1890) and the altar candles were not lit.[6] FHM had crept discreetly along the path of ceremonial, always alert to the reactions of the congregation.

My Dear Archbishop,

I have been requested to send to you, as our Diocesan, the accompanying memorial referring to the state of the Church of this Parish and the doctrines held by the Rector. The works alluded to are also sent herewith.

I may be permitted to state in explanation of the small number of signatures attached that no canvas has been thought desirable and the memorial emanates from those persons who feel themselves under the necessity of absenting themselves from their Parish Church for the reasons described in the Memorial.

I have reason to believe that there are many of the parishioners and heads of families who also disapprove of the proceedings of the Rector and object to the doctrines held by him, that (sic) who, for various reasons still attend the church.

I have the honour to remain, My Lord, your obedient and most faithful servant

SYDNEY

Together with the letter was the memorial signed by Lord Sydney and five others. It appealed to the Archbishop 'to restore the services of our church and the teaching of the clergy of this parish to that scriptural standard which is maintained in our Articles of Religion and Liturgy.' Also enclosed was a copy of FHM's leaflet *General Rules for the Guidance of Christian Life* which had been made available at the church.

Knowing of FHM's involvement with the SSC it is easy to see what prompted this leaflet: the section on Fasting, for example, comes straight from their Rule. 'Take less food than you are inclined to take: either by leaving off before you have quite satisfied your hunger or, if there are two kinds of food before you, by taking that which you like the least . . . Do not take so little food as in any way to impair your health, or attract needless remark.' This was probably the most extreme advice in the whole document but can hardly have merited a letter to the Archbishop.[7] However, there was another sentence which may have enraged Lord Sydney: 'If you cannot quiet your own conscience, or desire the special forgiveness of any sins, or require comfort and counsel, go to a Priest of God that you may receive the benefit of absolution and such

Emily, Countess Sydney. Photograph: G & R Lavis

spiritual advice as may be needful to you'. This was perilously close to advising 'Confession', a word guaranteed to provoke *frissons* of anti-Roman disgust.

The complaint mentioned in the memorial about the 'teaching' at St Nicholas' stemmed from a 'Eucharistic Manual' which had been given to the Confirmation candidates, most of them young people. In it, the Lord's Table was referred to as an 'Altar' (a word avoided by the Book of Common Prayer but not an illegal use) and the Priest as a 'sacrificing' Priest. The doctrine of the Real Presence was asserted.

For an evangelical like Lord Sydney these points were anathema and it is possible to understand his wish to stir up trouble. However, he did not set about it wisely. Firstly, he did not inform the Rector about the complaint and secondly, those he found to sign the memorial were hardly qualified to do so. One of them had not attended the church for seventeen years and the other four, two of whom were newcomers to the district, had never attended the church (except Mr White on two occasions).[8]

News that a memorial, critical of the Rector and intended for Archbishop Longley,[9] became known to some, including the Churchwardens, Messrs Janson and Charrington. Their loyal response was to gather signatures from twenty-four of the congregation and to frame a counter-memorial for the attention of the Rector: ' . . . and we therefore think it due to you that we should express our conviction that you neither hold nor have published any tenets inconsistent with the formularies of the Church of England. We avail ourselves of the present occasion to tender to you our respectful and affectionate acknowledgement of the privileges which under God's Providence we, in common with our fellow parishioners, enjoy through your ministry: as well as our sense of your increasing solicitude for the temporal welfare of the poorer members of your flock we rely upon your discretion for the avoidance of any changes in the present mode of celebrating Divine Service in the Parish Church which, although strictly legal might be calculated, by their adoption, to cause serious offence to the congregation.'

The Rector enjoyed strong approval from Lord Richard Cavendish, a Chislehurst resident and churchgoer, who wrote to the Archbishop on 9th February. He wished to bear witness to 'the anxious desire of the Rector not to offend even unreasonable prejudices on the part of any of his parishioners. Your Grace is, I believe, aware that no parish priest can be more devoted to his duties or perform them in a more exemplary manner than Mr Murray . . . I believe that personal animosity roused by wounded pride and disappointed love of domination is mainly at the bottom of the proceeding.'

Lord Richard Cavendish received a quick reply from the Archbishop and wrote back on 12th February: 'Lord Sydney I have known all my life and have never received anything but kindness from him but I cannot conceal from myself that he bears a strong personal grudge against Mr Murray. In the time of the late Rector, Lord Sydney's word was law and he has never been able to reconcile himself to a different state of things. He is moreover not very well-informed and has very strong prejudices on the subjects to which the memorial refers...'

The letters followed thick and fast: either Longley had become a particularly fine administrator since his disastrous days as Headmaster of Harrow School or this matter was attracting first rate attention because the complainant occupied the position of

Lord Chamberlain to the Queen.[10]

Lord Sydney wasted no time in asking his servants to hand over the 'pernicious' and 'objectionable' Confirmation booklets which they had received from the Rector; the Rector therefore requested their return to him. Lord and Lady Sydney withdrew their subscriptions from the local schools because 'they learned that I hold and teach the doctrine of The Real Presence which they consider to be contrary to the teaching of the reformed Church of England'.[11] The other memorialists followed suit. Lord and Lady Sydney withdrew also their subscription to the Shoe Club.[12]

FHM wrote to Lord Sydney on the matter of the Real Presence, concerned that he was confusing 'Real Presence' and 'Transubstantiation': perhaps the misunderstanding boiled down to a matter of terminology.

By now, the Rector had seen a copy of the memorial – it had been sent to him by the Archbishop – and it was time for him to respond in a letter to the Archbishop. In his own defence, the Rector wrote: '. . . it has been my most anxious and earnest endeavour, while teaching what I believe to be the doctrines of the Church, to maintain a medium line of services so as to satisfy, as far as I could, the general and various tastes and habits of person in these difficult and trying times.' He volunteered the suggestion that the Archbishop should send an observer, unannounced, to look at the services at St Nicholas' Church. In addition, he would be happy to come and see the Archbishop. 'I do not wish to be sacrificed to the views of the few.' He felt that the complaints about the services were too vague but made the point that services at St Nicholas' were so well attended that the people could hardly be accommodated. Along with a printed record of the previous year's communicant numbers and offerings he enclosed yet another tract explaining his stance on the Real Presence. This led to a separate argument, much protracted, between Longley and FHM with Longley making the accusation that FHM's views coincided with the Lutheran doctrine of 'consubstantiation'.

In March, just one month after the beginning of the episode, Longley replied to Lord Sydney's memorial. He had seen the counter-memorial and knew all the good points. He did not believe that there was dissatisfaction and could not find fault, legally, with the level of the ritualism. So far, so good (for the Rector), but the sting was in the tail. 'I must now avow that the Eucharistic manual does not reflect the mind of the Church of England . . . I am irresistibly led to the conclusion that the manual is so far from fairly reflecting the teaching of the Church of England, that it does in truth, harmonise in a much greater degree with the doctrine of the Church of Rome and virtually neutralises the Protest of the Church of England against those doctrines. I very strongly object therefore to its circulation in my diocese.'

This last point must have given satisfaction to the memorialists. Lord Sydney organised the printing of the original memorial and Longley's reply but there is no evidence of its circulation in Chislehurst. The matter was not referred to in the Parish Magazine because the magazine did not start publication until October of that year. However in January 1875, eight years later, the printed memorial again appeared in the Archbishop's file. Longley had died in 1868 and in November of that year Disraeli asked leave to nominate Dr Tait, the Bishop of London, as the next Archbishop of Canterbury.

Subsequent squalls in Chislehurst were to be settled by him.

* * *

Lord Sydney made a strong gesture of disapproval by involving himself in the establishment of a new church, Christchurch, in Lower Camden which was erected 'through the private liberality of a large body of the residents in Chislehurst and Bickley'.[13] It was Lady Sydney who laid the foundation stone in 1872 and the church, which was without its own ecclesiastical district, was consecrated by Archbishop Tait. The first incumbent was the Rev. William Fleming LL.B.

The picture would not be complete if mention were not made of the ill-feeling generated between these neighbouring clergy during the next few years. The facts have to be faced: FHM was building up a church with all the characteristics of the Anglo-Catholic movement while the new Christchurch was strongly evangelical. The Anglo-Catholics had a horror of the evangelicals' reliance on the scriptures and personal testimony while the evangelicals were even more horrified by the antics and Popery of the Anglo-Catholics. Without doubt there was some prejudice in each church.

Early in 1875 FHM was writing to the Archbishop of Canterbury: 'I object to the circulation of handbills in shops and houses of *my* parish inviting persons to attend services, Bible Classes, and classes for instruction in reading at Christchurch'. He assured Tait that he was not writing in an aggressive spirit but purely to establish a matter of order and prevailing custom between clergy. Fleming, in *his* letter to Tait, claimed that as it had no ecclesiastical district Christchurch was for the benefit of Chislehurst in general. However, he apologised for the intrusion. Tait finally pronounced that Fleming must not appear to be *inviting* FHM's congregation.

FHM was not going to give up that easily. His next letter informed the Archbishop of Fleming's public role in the laying of the foundation stone of the Wesleyan School and of Fleming's intention to take part in another non-conformist event during the next week. FHM felt aggrieved that the Church of England was, in this instance, appearing on the same platform as Dissenters. With a hint of impatience, Tait maintained that he could not interfere 'for Church of England Clergymen are given a large liberty in deciding what ought to be their bearing towards Wesleyans and Dissenters'.

In case this should be seen as a hagiographic study of FHM, this may be the moment to question his methods. It is not possible to know the level of Fleming's intrusion over the three years since the opening of Christchurch but had FHM tried negotiating with Fleming before writing to Tait? Was the congregation of St Nicholas' troubled by Christchurch publicity or was there indeed animosity between the two churches? Without its own district, how could Christchurch legitimately cast its net?[14] For incumbents like FHM and Fleming who were attempting to get across a certain 'brand' of the faith, the parish system was usually a natural protection of boundaries. It would certainly be expected that neighbouring clergy would not actively poach from each other.

The tale-telling on the support given by Fleming to the Wesleyans is understandable but now seems rather self-righteous. In his defence, a conservative like FHM would have been conscious of slights to the Established Church and might have felt it his duty to report any cases of fraternisation. Ecumenism existed but had not, in general, 'caught on' at local levels.

December 1876 saw the next confrontation: the evidence gives a clear opportunity for reading between the lines. It was decided that St Nicholas' Church should organise a mission. This would be an intense week of services using visiting preachers: endeavours would be made to cater for all sorts of people at the hours most suited to each. At FHM's request the Archbishop provided a few words to be used in publicity, warmly endorsing the mission and its aims.

By the end of the week the Archbishop had received an indignant letter from some Christchurch members protesting against the way in which the Chislehurst mission had been conducted. They had been induced to attend by the Rector's invitation, the Archbishop's approval and by the Rector's verbal assurance that the pure and simple Gospel alone would be proclaimed. They had been assured by the Rector himself that the services would be such that all church people, and 'our Wesleyan neighbours too', might cordially join in them.

'Notwithstanding a distinct warning from our own clergyman [Fleming] on the previous Sunday, we, as teachers of our several Bible classes decided to go and judge for ourselves still hoping the teaching would prove unobjectionable and such as would be *helpful* rather than *hurtful* to the members of our classes, all of whom had been invited to attend the mission.

'We went last Wednesday evening and to our surprise and intense indignation personal and habitual confession to the *priest* was not merely defended but distinctly enjoined and insisted upon . . .

'We will only add that so far from pointing anxious souls to the One Great High Priest . . . it seems to point away from him and rather to the poor earthly priest so often arrogant and frail from whom, in these days of general education and an open English Bible, may God in his mercy defend our country and our happy English homes!'

No doubt wearily, the Archbishop picked up his pen: 'My Dear Mr Murray, I have received the enclosed letter and should be much obliged if, bearing in mind the letter which I sent to you authorising the mission in your parish, you would send me such an explanation as I can make use of in answer to this correspondent.'

FHM, in reply, felt that the mission had gone well. He reminded the Archbishop that, in conversation, he had once said that confession was not obligatory but that he had no objection. 'Confession is a means of grace.' The Archbishop presented FHM with a document entitled *The Bishops' Report on Confession* (1873).

Fortunately for FHM the Rural Dean had been present at the service in which the controversial sermon had been preached by a visiting clergyman: he could see no problem. FHM was asked to take a copy of the sermon to the Archbishop at Addington Palace.

The final reply from the Archbishop to the Christchurch complainants started with a sentence which was weighted heavily with past experience. 'As is not unusual in such cases, I have found that the impression conveyed to you by the sermon in question, which I understand to have been delivered extempore, is very different from the construction put upon it by Mr Murray.' From the evidence he had seen (that is, the reconstructed extempore sermon) the Archbishop could not condemn the sermon.

To put the complaint to rest, Mr Fleming also was presented with a copy of *The Bishops' Report on Confession.* The reasons for the emergence of this report, three years previously, are covered in Chapter 14.

The Bishops' Report on Confession 23rd July 1873

The opening paragraph pointed out that Penance could not be counted as a true Sacrament of the Gospel: this statement was derived from the twenty fifth Article of Religion. The Bishops did not recognise the words Sacrament of Confession but they conceded that in the services there was provision for Public Confession and Absolution yet, for the relief of troubled consciences the Church had made two exceptions.

1. In the case of those with unquiet consciences previous to receiving Holy Communion the minister can say 'Let him come to me or to some other discreet and learned Minister of God's Word and open his grief that by the ministry of God's Holy Word he may receive the benefit of Absolution together with Ghostly Counsel and Advice.' In such case no form of Absolution has been prescribed in the Book of Common Prayer and further the rubric in the 1549 Prayer Book which sanctioned a particular form of Absolution has been withdrawn from subsequent editions.

2. Visitation of the Sick. A sick person may be moved to make a special confession if he feels his conscience troubled. This does not authorise the clergy to require the sick to open their grief, or enumerate their sins or to require private confession arrangements or to give the impression it attains a higher spiritual life.

---

1 This is not to say that the ritualism controversy had gone away altogether: this was to be a battlefield for nearly another 50 years.

2 Alexander Pope, *Imitations of Horace. Book 2.*

3 The Chislehurst families are riddled with Albinias as will be seen by the memorials in the Scadbury Chapel: for more information see *The Albinia Book* by Albinia Lucy Wherry (1929).

4 The Selwyn family is another thread embroidered into the Chislehurst tapestry. The Chantrey monument on the South wall commemorates a Selwyn. The founder of Selwyn College, Cambridge, is of this family.

5 Archaeologia Cantiana vol. 13 *'Chislehurst and its Church'.*

6 The ornaments rubric of the 1549 Prayer Book had allowed candles as long as they were used only for light.

7 Other points were: 'Spend Sunday holily, cheerfully – it is not to be a gloomy day . . . but indulge no noisy mirth or games and do no unnecessary work upon it. Attend church regularly twice in the day if possible . . . Be regular in receiving the Blessed Sacrament . . . Always communicate early in the morning before you have taken any food . . .'

8 These facts were passed on to the Archbishop in the counter-memorial which was to follow.

9 Longley, as described in Chapter 3, had been FHM's headmaster at Harrow School.

10 It is interesting to see the Archbishop's letters which were scrawled on blue foolscap paper as an initial draft and then corrected by crossings out and insertions: it is these corrected letters which were kept in the file. Presumably, fair copies were sent to the contestants in Chislehurst.

11 Letter from FHM to the Archbishop.

12 One of the many Chislehurst charities for the poor.

13 Webb, Miller, Beckwith, *A History of Chislehurst.*

14 Christchurch soon developed into a flourishing church. Within seven years, enlargement was needed because of the growing population of the area. A splendid Father Willis organ was installed in 1873. Parish boundaries were established in 1906 but, interestingly, pew rents were not abolished until 1968.

Chapter 11

The Church of the Annunciation to the Blessed Virgin Mary

We hope to build a little chapel here for the overflowing of our church – or rather more correctly, to serve for an outlying part of the parish from whence the people find it difficult to come as often as might be desired and to leave them no excuse. This is the best testimony to the value of dear FM's exertions; for when he first came about 120 people used to come to morning service in great square boxes – so high that they could scarcely see each other and now there is not room for them to sit in the closely managed low seats although I believe there are 500 sittings. We are therefore endeavouring to provide this additional little temple which, although not to be consecrated by a bishop, will send up prayers unto the Good Shepherd without any burden on others, but it comes just at the moment when we have to make up a deficiency of £500 for the restoration of the tower, steeple, bells etc. from the effect of the fire [Chapter 7], and many of the most zealous have exhausted themselves, and the richest of the inhabitants, being prejudiced against the doctrines being fairly preached and all in perfect accordance with the Church of England and with primitive truth, will not give their mite.

Many withhold conscientiously, as the saying is, and it is to be hoped that the time will come in their case as it has happily done with many others when they will appreciate the blessedness of what is within their reach. Until then we must go on in love but without them. If therefore, my dear, you can spare £5 for our little work, I know it will gratify my dear boy and give us aid in a good cause.

A letter from JOHN ANDERDON *in March 1858*
on the matter of a chapel at Prickend.

The developing need for a Chapel of Ease in Prickend can be traced. Both socially and geographically Chislehurst was a two tier society: the area around St Nicholas' contained the residences of the well-to-do and Prickend, down a slight hill, catered for the dependent servants and artisans. There is a myth current in Chislehurst that alternative provision for worship was necessary because the well-to-do resented sharing their worship with the lower classes. There is absolutely no evidence to support this story. Indeed the other side of the coin ought to be looked at. The people of Prickend faced a double disincentive to attend church: not only was it a long haul on foot to get up to St Nicholas' but also it was necessary to have a 'Sunday Best' and the means of sprucing up in order to join the intimidating congregation. It was *they* who had difficulties in sharing their worship with the affluent. No situation could have shouted more loudly for a Chapel of Ease which, by definition, is one which is provided for the 'ease and comfort' of those living at some distance from the parish church.

Originally, the Rev. George Cosby White, from 1853 to1856, took services in a cottage in Prickend and after he left Mr Dumbleton took over. It soon became apparent that larger premises were needed and so contributions were solicited. £250 was raised to build a small chapel which can still be seen in Queen Street, no longer now a place of worship. The chapel, which was described by *The Bromley Record* as a 'school-chapel', had room for 120 worshippers and was designed by Mr Wollaston.

However there then followed a marked expansion in the population of Prickend and the need for a substantial church became apparent: here was an opportunity for the Rector to build a church which satisfied his vision architecturally and which would contain the ornaments and style which he was aiming for at St Nicholas'. The anniversary celebrations of the Chapel of Ease were held on 21st November, 1867, and the Parish Magazine optimistically noted that these would probably be the last such celebrations because of the creation of the new church. The Chapel of Ease was to become an Infants' School.

The site for the new church had been provided by the generosity of Mr Slade of Kemnal Manor, John Anderdon and Miss Sanders, the stepdaughter of the Rector. Bishop Jenner laid the foundation stone in 1868. Unfortunately many difficulties were experienced in securing good foundations and costs began to rise beyond the estimate. Rescue came with a donation from Miss Paterson, a relative of Mrs Murray, and also from the Rector's significant contributions which derived from the profits of *Hymns Ancient and Modern*. The dedication of the new church had been inspired by FHM's visit to a Church of the Annunciation in Florence. With this choice, FHM was skating on thin ice for this was probably the first such dedication since before the Reformation and it gave rise to disapproval in some quarters. However, 'The Church of the Annunciation to the Blessed Virgin Mary' was approved by Archbishop Longley just before he died in October 1868 and the church was finally ready for consecration, except for the South Chapel and tower,[1] by 25th October 1870. Dr Tait, formerly Bishop of London, succeeded Longley.

The architect was Mr James Brooks. A contemporary judgement in the Parish Magazine expressed the general admiration for the new church which, as can still be seen, has something about it which lifts it above the ordinary: 'Mr Brooks is certainly to be congratulated . . . so noble a building, one which by its beautiful proportions, massive grandeur, and yet sober, unpretentious character, has an inspiring effect on all who enter it'.

* * *

It was clearly intended that members of the St Nicholas' congregation should be prepared to change their place of worship if they lived nearer to the Church of the

Annunciation. Earlier in 1870 Thomas Charrington had made a statement in the Parish Magazine about the difficulties of seating the congregation at St Nicholas'. 'The churchwardens wish it to be understood that they do not authorise the occupation of seats by non-parishioners before the commencement of the services, to the exclusion of the inhabitants; neither do they approve of the seats, which have been regularly occupied by the older residents, being taken possession of by those who have come into the parish more recently and they will therefore be willing to receive applications from any parishioners who are not at present provided with sittings and will endeavour to seat them according to seniority of residence. It is anticipated that those who live nearer the new Church of the Annunciation (which will be opened for Divine Service, probably in the Autumn) will attend the services of that church.'

However, there was a policy to ensure a continuity of social contacts between the two congregations. This was summed up at a later date: 'In reality there would not be any division, the Parish would remain one in feeling, in clubs, schools, charities, etc.'[2]

On 26th October 1871, almost exactly one year later, St Nicholas' and her daughter church shared their first Dedication Day. Judging from the account in the Parish Magazine this must have been an astonishing occasion. Not only were there extra church services in each place and magnificent processions of choir and augmented clergy but also there was a fine lunch in the Village Hall: indeed, such were the numbers that there had to be two sittings. And then, after lunch the fun began. The idea seems to have been to propose a toast to – well, just everyone! The Queen and members of the Royal Family; the Emperor Napoleon, Empress Eugénie and the Prince Imperial; the Archbishop of Canterbury; all the visiting clergy. Bishop Jenner then proposed the health of the Rector and this 'elicited the heartiest reception'. Mr Janson proposed the health of the Curates who each replied and then it was the turn of the churchwardens, Mr Janson and Mr Charrington, who also replied with brief speeches. Mr Janson rose again to propose the health of the visitors. The Rev. Charles Lowder was, of course, present and having spoken on behalf of the visitors he proposed a toast to the choirs to which the respective organists gave response. Then came the health of the parishioners which was acknowledged by Lord Richard Cavendish. Up stood the Rector and gave the health of the school teachers, Mr and Mrs Eggleton and their two assistants. Mr Eggleton, with a few well-chosen words, gave thanks and gave way to Mr Torre who proposed the health of the bellringers: their response came from Mr Stanley Wollaston. Lastly, the Rector proposed the health of Bishop Jenner, offering as a plea for the lateness of this toast that the place of honour for a Bishop in a procession is always at the end. The Bishop who was also welcomed as an old parishioner, responded by proposing 'the ladies' and asking Mr Charrington to make response on their behalf.

'The repast was provided, as usual, by various parishioners who liberally responded to the call made upon them for a supply of the necessary joints of meat &c. &c. to furnish the tables.' What was not made clear was the nature of the liquid refreshment provided for all of those toasts. Perhaps it was tea.

In the evening the two congregations joined together again for a festal Evening

by courtesy of the National Portrait Gallery, London

Henry Jenner, Bishop of Dunedin 1866-1871. Photograph: M. Jacolette.

Prayer at the Annunciation where, it was recorded, there was a choir of fifty men and boys who were, without exception, parishioners.

Sadly, the next year's Dedication Day was postponed and subdued because of the news that the younger son of John Anderdon had died suddenly at Henlade House. 'All in the parish entertain respectful feelings to those on whom this great sorrow has fallen. Of their self-denying charity and Christian labours the Orphanage is but one evidence but many a heart amongst our poorer neighbours knows more than we do of that kind and liberal sympathy which was always ready to be bestowed when occasion for it arises . . .'

* * *

At this time there was a spurt of provision for religious observance in Chislehurst. The Parish Church had of course occupied a central position for centuries and the Prickend Chapel of Ease was built in 1859. There came a number of additions: the Roman Catholic Church of St Mary in 1853, both the Wesleyan Church[3] and the Church of the Annunciation in 1870 and, as has been noted, Christchurch in 1872 (Chapter 10). There was therefore an opportunity for all shades of worship in Chislehurst.

FHM, realising how precarious the Tractarian presence was in Chislehurst, had long cherished the idea that the Annunciation 'district' should be upgraded to a 'parish' in its own right and that, in some way, the patronage could be arranged so that the continuity of the Catholic ideal could be ensured. The parlous state of the Church of England in the 1870s will be covered in Chapter 13. The 1874 Dedication Day repeated the extravaganza of previous years, this time with at least 26 clergy: Charles Lowder and Bishop Jenner were again present and also FHM's brother Frederick from Stone, near Dartford. The main celebration of Holy Communion was followed by the customary 'feast' and the, by now, customary toasts and speeches. The Parish Magazine gave the following summary indicating the tone of the speeches: 'It was impossible that such a meeting could pass without many allusions to the great crisis through which the church is at present passing, and to the prospect of a religious persecution in England in the year 1875. The necessity of churchmen adhering firmly and faithfully to the principles of the Prayer Book and of resisting all Parliamentary interference with the doctrine or the worship of the church was urged. It would indeed be a deplorable calamity to the nation if the Prayer Book, which was finally revised and put forth with all due authority in 1662, were tampered with or altered in opposition to those who have learnt to love and make use of it.'

In November 1874 meetings of parishioners were held as preliminaries to the task of raising subscriptions for the proposed ecclesiastical separation of the Church of the Annunciation and the necessary endowment fund: Mr Jackson, one of the Annunciation Treasurers, had already received donations.

On 1st February 1875, the Village Hall was crowded for an important meeting to launch the Endowment Fund officially, the agreement having been obtained from the Ecclesiastical Commissioners and all the relevant church dignitaries. The detailed account in the Parish Magazine reports the Rector's justification for the proposed course of action for he had been accused of acting in a 'hole in corner' manner.

Firstly, he said that the scheme had his support because 'it concerned the religious welfare of the parish'. His next point was about the cost to himself: it was with considerable difficulty that he provided the stipends of the assistant clergy and he could not expect a successor to do as much pecuniarily as God had permitted him to do. On the question of patronage he explained that it was customary for the incumbent of the parish to have the first presentation but, after that, he was quite willing for the subscribers to decide whether the patronage should be in the hands of trustees or in a public body. There had been unpleasant accusations that the Rector wished to retain the patronage for himself and thus to promulgate Romish doctrines. These accusations had come from the Lord Sydney faction in the form of *another* memorial to the Archbishop of Canterbury. Of the thirty four signatories twenty were known to attend Christchurch, seven were Wesleyans (including their minister) and two had left the parish but still retained property in Chislehurst.

by permission of Roger Long

The Church of the Annunciation. Photograph: Roy Patey

Lord Sydney put Archbishop Tait 'into the picture' by sending him a copy of his predecessor's response to the 1867 memorial, highlighting the last paragraph which, referring to the Confirmation booklet, had said: 'So far from fairly reflecting the teaching of the Church of England it does, in truth harmonise in a much greater degree with that of the Church of Rome and virtually neutralises the Protest of the Church of England against those doctrines'. In Lord Sydney's preamble to the 1874 memorial he complained that it was only by chance that he had heard that it was proposed to form a new ecclesiastical district for the Annunciation and that, when constituted, the patronage would be vested in perpetuity in trustees or a public body to be nominated in either case by the Rector. 'We view with serious apprehension the proposed nomination of the trustees by the present Rector as an attempt to perpetuate in the parish the ritualistic doctrines, teaching and practices, some of which were brought to the attention of the late Archbishop . . . We have every reason to believe that Mr Murray's public and private teaching has undergone no change since that time and it would be a grievous injury to the parish if it were to be made permanent.' The memorialists sought to influence His Grace to protect Chislehurst against the Rector's ways and they asked him to withhold his consent.

In reply the Archbishop agreed that, at first sight, it would not seem that the population of Chislehurst (2,600) merited the presence of three large churches but it was necessary to look at future expansion: 'It is my duty to be beforehand in making suitable provision . . .' He confessed that he had already given consent as long as £3,000 was raised to form a permanent endowment and he would not advise 'yes' until this condition had been complied with. Tait agreed that Lord Sydney had a good point about the Romanising influence 'but it is a grave charge against the first incumbent (as yet unknown) or the trustees'.

There was, of course, a counter-memorial, signed by 480 people, and at a public meeting of 350 the scheme was supported unanimously. In all the correspondence that followed, the Archbishop's tone towards FHM was markedly conciliatory and sympathetic.

At FHM's request Tait agreed to allow his letters in support of the Rector to be published in the Parish Magazine. He stated that FHM's willingness to hand over the patronage of the Church of the Annunciation to Keble College, Oxford, would go a long way towards quietening the original memorialists and he covered the problem of Romish ways by this final sentence: 'I feel assured from our conversation that it is by no means your wish to revive in either of your churches what is commonly called the Doctrine of the Mass, or to encourage your people to such an adoration of the sacramental bread and wine as has been declared by our Church to be "Idolatry to be abhorred of all faithful Christians" '.

In fact, FHM had come out of this latest spat quite well: he had the Archbishop's approval for the ecclesiastical division of the parish of St. Nicholas', he was able to broadcast the Archbishop's confidence on the matter of his doctrinal views and what might have seemed like the constraint of vesting patronage in Keble College was nothing of the sort. Keble College had been founded in only 1870 but, as its very name suggests, it was a bastion of Tractarianism. It had been founded in memory of John Keble whose sermon, it will be remembered, had marked the start of the Oxford Movement (Chapter 4). He himself had never sought preferment and, in spite of brilliant achievements at Oxford, he had spent his ministry with the people of the small parish of Hursley, near Winchester. He contributed to the *Tracts for the Times* and therein made a forceful appeal to the clergy to take a high view of their privileges and duties. His life and work bore out these ideals. Until his death in 1866 he maintained the Catholicity of the Church of England.

The patronage of the Church of the Annunciation could not have been in safer hands. The Endowment Committee wasted no time. In fact, even before the Archbishop's opinions were known, discreet enquiries were arriving on the desk of the Rev. Edward Talbot, the first Warden of Keble College. Mr Jackson's first letter, dated 2nd February 1875, raised the issue of securing Catholic-minded incumbents for the Church of the Annunciation for all time. He laid down the condition that the Rev. H.L. Russell, the then Curate-in-Charge, should be appointed first incumbent and asked 'Would you also kindly let me know what security is provided, in the constitution of the Council [of Keble College] for its always being composed of men of the school of thought to which the late J. Keble belonged as this would be a most material point with us'.

Apart from a firm refusal from Keble College to a request to add to the Endowment Fund (understandable because the college was both new and short of endowments itself) matters evolved with tolerable satisfaction although Keble College did not show quite the enthusiasm that had been hoped for.[4] The formal letter vesting the Patronage of the Church of the Annunciation in the College was sent out by the Ecclesiastical Commissioners on the 3rd August 1875.

Finally, in December 1875 the Rev. H.L. Russell became the first Vicar of the Parish of the Annunciation to the Blessed Virgin Mary.

---

1 Many thought that the whole edifice should have been completed there and then but FHM was adamant that the cost of the building should not exceed the money raised. The South Chapel was not finished until 1885 when the foundations for the tower were laid as well.

2 Parish Magazine 1874.

3 The Wesleyan Church in Chislehurst, a fine Gothic structure looking very much like a new Anglican church, was soon to become a church of some importance. Of the first six ministers, three became President of Conference. In 1881 its two chief office bearers were Robert Perks, subsequently the leading Nonconformist Liberal in the Commons and eventually a baronet and G.H. Chubb, of the lock and safe company, the promoter of the Nonconformist Unionist Association and eventually a peer. D.W. Bebbington, *The non-Conformist Conscience, Chapel and Politics, 1870-1914.*

4 They were certainly obstructive when it came to taking responsibility for the Vicarage which had been built as a result of voluntary subscription in 1896/7.

Chapter 12

Death at Sea

At midnight there was a cry made

From the memorial to HERBERT MURRAY *in Chislehurst churchyard.*

(Matthew 25.6)

It was only about six weeks before the consecration of the Church of the Annunciation in October 1870 that FHM heard the dreadful news that his younger son, Herbert, had been drowned at sea at the age of twenty. This was particularly poignant for it was the birth of Herbert which had led to the death of FHM's first wife Fanny. Her sister, Anne, wrote of the grief suffered by the Rector in 1870: 'The stunning blow did nearly crush / the stricken father to the dust'.

Herbert had started his naval career at the age of fourteen in *HMS Aurora.* His log book was written up in exquisite handwriting and the confident pencil sketches show places he visited, such as Barbados and Dominica. For someone aged between fourteen and sixteen years of age his entries sound remarkably authoritative: 'Received intelligence that the Stoker was found dead on the beach . . . sent funeral party on shore to inter the remains' or 'Read warrants to Wm Whiting to reduce him to second class and Wm Booth for confinement in cells for 178 hours'.

On his next cruise in the *Aurora* he went from Cape Hitian to Port Royal and after that a cruise which took in Alexandria and Constantinople. The faithfully maintained log books survive in pristine condition.

At some time in 1870 he joined *HMS Captain* under the distinguished Capt. Hugh Talbot Burgoyne. Burgoyne had gained a very early Victoria Cross: in 1855 he had taken a party on land during the Crimean War and successfully set fire to Russian stores. He was awarded the VC when it was instituted in 1857.

* * *

The *Captain* was put in commission on 30th April 1870. *The Times* newspaper of those days was surprisingly open about the construction details and movements of ships and, making the assumption that he took that newspaper, FHM would have had the pleasure of following his son's activities at a distance. Indeed, the *Captain* was singularly newsworthy because of its controversial design: its originality was such that the designer Capt. Cowper Phipps Coles found himself in direct confrontation with the Admiralty, especially in the person of the Chief Constructor for the Admiralty, Sir Edward James Reed.

The situation regarding the development of warships at that time can be briefly summed up as follows: warships constructed totally of wood had disappeared entirely and their successors, the hybrid 'wooden-ironclads' were abandoned by the mid-1860s; France led the way in the building of totally ironclad warships; the Crimean

HMS Captain underway in rough seas.

War had underlined the need for shallow draught warships mounting one or two heavy guns for bombardment. These needed to be small and fast with all-round fire so that they were well adapted for breaking into the ports and harbours of an enemy. On the other hand they needed to be ocean-going vessels in order to reach their destinations and to function in any engagement on open seas. The all-round fire was achieved by a brilliant idea credited to Capt. Coles but claimed also by an American named Ericsson. It has furthermore been suggested that Isambard Kingdom Brunel originally put the idea to Coles.[1]

The innovation was based on the simple idea that instead of having to manoeuvre the whole ship in order to point the guns at a target, the guns alone should be moved. The circle of fire was to be achieved by swivelling turrets at each end of the deck.

The Admiralty, understandably wary of such a radical departure from previous designs, allowed the use of turrets to creep in but Coles pressed for a ship that would incorporate not only the turrets but also an exceptionally low freeboard of eight feet. In addition he aimed at a combination of steam power and sail – to be used separately or in partnership. The proposed ship, to be known as the *Captain*, was seen by Coles as a serious rival to the much vaunted but more conventional turret ship the *Monarch*, designed by Sir Edward Reed. The Admiralty had confidently commissioned the *Monarch* but not the, as yet unrealised, *Captain*. Coles was therefore forced to proceed alone. At his own expense the *Captain* was built by Messrs Laird of Birkenhead: it was to be the only battleship ever to be privately designed and financed on behalf of the

Royal Navy. 'The building of a new ship [the *Captain*] was definitely authorised on 23rd July 1866, notwithstanding the submission of the Controller of the navy [Sir Ernest Reed] that it was doubtful whether the proposed height of freeboard [eight feet] would be satisfactory for a sea-going cruising ship . . . That she should be considered to the fullest extent a sea-going cruising ship was Coles's earnest intention and he was supported by such a weight of public opinion that the Admiralty, laying the responsibility on Coles and the Lairds, sanctioned her being commissioned . . . although it was found that the freeboard was less, by nearly two feet than had been designed.'[2]

* * *

'Public opinion' is an interesting aspect of this whole affair for it reveals how concerned with naval affairs were the people of Victorian Britain: Sir Ernest Reed saw Coles as an amateur asserting himself against the authority and expertise of the Admiralty whereas the public saw him as a hero making a stand. Coles was so engrossed by the question of defensive armour for ships that from 1856 onwards he had devoted himself to its study at his own cost and, for most of the time, on half pay. Coles had received encouragement from Prince Albert himself and after her husband's death, Queen Victoria continued to show her support.

Another noteworthy point is the Admiralty's acceptance of the fact that the freeboard was eventually only six feet, not eight feet. The risk attached to such a mistake was not considered. However, to his credit, having resigned his office as Chief Constructor for the Admiralty in July 1870, Sir Ernest Reed did speak out: his resignation had been due to disagreements over the handling of the turret ships controversy.

HMS Captain: one of the two turrets

In a long and forceful letter to *The Times* of 8th August 1870 he defended the Admiralty against public opinion which believed that the Admiralty had set its face against the idea of ironclad turret ships: 'This is only one of the perpetually recurring instances in which outside persons, in the absence of official information, do great injustice to the servants of the Crown and the country'. He criticised the design of the *Captain* at length comparing it with his own design for the *Monarch* which, although using the turret innovation, was a heavier and higher vessel (the *Monarch* was used as the *Captain's* 'sparring partner' in the trials taking place that summer).

He was especially virulent on the matter of the miscalculations that had occurred: 'Captain Coles has supervised the *Captain* and has had his way absolutely and the consequence is what I have already mentioned – namely, the very worst failure in a ship to fulfil her design that I have ever known . . . her side is six feet high and would have been eight feet but for an alarming blunder in calculation . . . 800 or 900 tons too heavy . . . promised that she could carry about 1,100 tons of coal but she can only take 500 or 600 tons with her other stores on board . . . It is satisfactory to know that in spite of these drawbacks the *Captain* has proved capable of going to sea . . .'

* * *

Compare this letter with reports in *The Times* a few weeks earlier. For example, on 29th July: 'The ocean-going frigate *Captain* anchored at Spithead yesterday after a most successful three weeks' experimental cruise in steaming and sailing...and gunnery practice. Captain Coles was on board as a guest of Captain Burgoyne... Although carrying an enormous load of armour and armament she tacks under sail around a supposed antagonist as handily as one of our old yet quick-moving frigates ... Everyone does his work without the slightest hindrance to the rest and five minutes after the bugle sounds everyone is at his post and engaged in the attack. It is perfectly just to all concerned to mention that the *Monarch* turret ship cannot be fought in this way.'

And then on 1st August: 'The ocean-going frigate *Captain* has gone into Portsmouth Harbour to take in coal to prepare for her coming cruise with the *Monarch* and the Channel Fleet. She has no defects of any kind to make good and is in magnificent order in-board . . . it is generally thought that a ship with a high freeboard must of necessity be a much drier ship at sea in all weathers than a ship with a low freeboard . . . This is the case with a heavy beam sea running but under every other condition the *Captain* [low freeboard] is every bit as dry as the *Monarch* [high freeboard]. As a proof of the steadiness and dryness of the *Captain*, on the whole of the voyage out between Plymouth and Vigo . . . the turret was used by the men to clean their arms, to smoke upon and as a general promenade to those off duty. . . Steaming across the Bay of Biscay allowed a check on the ventilation and the impression is that the *Captain* is pre-eminently a cool ship below . . . Under steam or under sail the ship has proved wonderfully easy in all her movements and under sail alone has been tacked with a certainty of answering her helm . . . no matter how slow the speed.' Coles himself said: 'She walks the water like a thing of life'.

by permission of Cdr Nigel Anderdon

Survivors of the *Captain*

After these rapturous descriptions at the beginning of August, Sir Edward Reed's letter a week later must have seemed incomprehensible.

* * *

On 10th September: 'The news of a dreadful calamity reached London yesterday evening. *Her Majesty's Ship Captain* has foundered off Finisterre. Nothing has been found of her but for boats and some spars. Her crew of 500 hands must all have perished . . . The ship was commanded by some of the finest officers in the Navy but her able inventor, Capt. Cowper Coles, was also on board and has perished in the vessel which realised the long-delayed triumph of his genius.'

It emerged that there was, in fact, a total of eighteen survivors who escaped in a launch and it is to them and a report by Admiral Milne (who was in an accompanying ship) that we owe the brief description of events. Captain Burgoyne acted as a heroic captain should: he refused the chance to join the eighteen men in case he should prove one too many for the small boat.

Admiral Milne of the *Lord Warden* had visited the *Captain* on the morning of 6th September and inspected her minutely. As the day progressed the winds increased, 'at 8 and 10pm there was no indication of a heavy gale . . . at 11 the breeze began to freshen with rain. Towards midnight the barometer had fallen . . . before 1am the gale had set in at S.W. At 1.15am the *Captain* was sailing astern of the *Lord Warden*. Until 1.30 I constantly watched the ship . . . she was heeling over a good deal to starboard with the wind on her port side . . . her red bow light was all this time clearly seen. Some minutes after I again looked for her light but it was thick with rain and the light was no longer visible. The squalls of wind and rain were very heavy and on the *Lord Warden* it was thought the sea would have broken over her gangways.' By 2.25 the gale had somewhat subsided and the stars came out clear and bright. 'No large ship was seen near us . . . the *Captain* was missing.' The remaining ten of the eleven ships of the fleet conducted a thorough search which found only wreckage and one body.

The survivors' experiences appeared in *The Times* of 14th September. It was soon after midnight that the angle of heel began to increase rapidly towards a complete capsize. The effect in the boiler room was to break open the furnace doors through which poured the burning coals: the incoming sea produced scalding steam such as to skin the men alive. Those who escaped successfully (another boat was seen bottom upwards) reached Concubion.

The news of the sinking of the *Captain* would have first reached the families of the victims through the pages of the newspaper. The possibility of a vessel of the proportions of the *Captain* succumbing to the violence of the sea was doubted by all and in Plymouth and Devonport (the ship was largely manned by West Country men) newspaper offices were surrounded by crowds waiting for confirmation.

The disaster, however, was a national event. The court martial bleakly concluded that the *Captain* was top heavy. Sir Edward Reed could be forgiven if he preened himself a little on his foresight and informed criticism of the design of the *Captain*.

In Chislehurst, Herbert Murray was mourned by many with a personal sorrow: 'Born and brought up in the parish, there is a large circle of young persons to whom as playmate, companion or friend he had specially endeared himself and who, as we know, mourn his loss as that of a dear brother'.[3] His stone memorial by the south east corner of St Nicholas' Church shows an anchor, said to be a copy of the *Captain's* anchor. There is also a memorial east window in the Church of the Annunciation as well as a window and brass tablet at St Nicholas'. FHM chose to put some words from a Keble poem onto the churchyard memorial:

> *'Death only binds us fast to the bright shore of love'*
>
> JOHN KEBLE

Napoleon III

A coincidence provides a footnote to this disaster. The pages of *The Times* which tell of the last days of the *Captain* also carry the latest from Paris on the Franco-Prussian War. The controversy about the *Captain* continued in The Times throughout the month of September in which time the Emperor surrendered to the Prussians (2nd September) and suffered a reverse in popularity. From *The Times* of 10th September: 'Portraits are destroyed, busts thrown into the streets . . . statues dragged from their pedestals and dashed to pieces and the very name of Napoleon, but a little while ago a bulwark of strength to the nation is a word of execration in every man's mouth'.

5th September: ' . . .The Empress Eugénie left France yesterday via Mauberge. Her son with his suite passed through the same town that evening.'

10th September: 'The Prince Imperial is now taking daily exercise on the promenade at Hastings.'

On 20th September the Empress and the Prince Imperial moved to Camden Place in Chislehurst. The residence had been made ready for just such an eventuality.

21st September: 'The Emperor Napoleon's horses were sold at auction . . . They were described as the property of a nobleman . . . the Imperial arms had been painted out . . .'

28th September: 'Her Majesty the Queen addressed a letter of sympathy to the Empress.'

It was on 20th March 1871 that Napoleon III, having been released by the Prussians, landed in Dover to an enthusiastic welcome: he travelled thence to Chislehurst where he died in 1873. Chislehurst was enthusiastic in support of the Imperial family, appreciative of the generosity of their presence. In spite of the fact that the Napoleonic royal family was, of course, devoutly Roman Catholic, FHM was drawn into the Imperial circle: 'When the Emperor Napoleon and Empress Eugénie lived at Chislehurst, Mr Murray was *persona grata* at Camden Place, and he was one of the three Anglican clergy present at the funeral of the Emperor'.[4] The Emperor's obituary in the Parish Magazine was an honest appraisal of his virtues and shortcomings.[5]

There is an anecdote recorded by Henry Vizetelly,[6] a journalist who had covered the war and the siege of Paris. He had been at school in Chislehurst in the 1830s and after a fleeting visit in the 1870s lamented the changes he found: 'The church had been more or less Romanised . . . and in the trim kept churchyard the newer graves were scarcely visible under their chaplets and clusters of flowers . . . As I stood pondering over the many changes which the past forty years had brought about, the exiled Emperor and Empress of the French, and the young Prince Louis, attended by some members of their suite, passed on foot through the gilded gateway of Camden Place to the Common where a small crowd of well-dressed sycophants were assembled to receive them with that blind obsequious homage which our tuft-hunting British race invariably accords to rank . . . I could not but feel that most of the grave disasters which had befallen France had their origin in that Imperial rule so much belauded by English people . . .'

1 Coles' obituary in *The Times* of 12th September 1870.

2 Capt. Cowper Coles: *The Dictionary of National Biography*.

3 Parish Magazine, October 1870.

4 Canterbury Diocesan Gazette, *Obituary of Canon Murray*, November 1902.

5 For a fuller account of the Bonaparte family's time in Chislehurst see Tom Bushell, *Imperial Chislehurst.*

6 Henry Vizetelly, *Glances back through Seventy Years.*

Chapter 13

The 1870s – the Church of England becomes a Battleground

Lord, we beseech thee, let thy continual pity cleanse and defend thy Church; and because it cannot continue in safety without thy succour, preserve it evermore by thy help and goodness; through Jesus Christ our Lord. Amen.

Collect for the Sixteenth Sunday after Trinity

Imminent threats to the Church of England have already been hinted at. In the speeches at the Dedication Festival of the Church of the Annunciation in 1874 phrases such as 'great crisis' and 'religious persecution' were understood by all present and needed no further explanation. Not only was the issue a persistent theme in the newspapers but also, in the previous month, there had been a detailed article in the Parish Magazine, composed probably by one of FHM's curates, reminding the congregation of what was meant by 'Catholic and Protestant'. This ensured that when battle lines were drawn up it would be clear where Chislehurst stood – to be accurate, just St Nicholas' and The Annunciation because FHM had already weathered a Protestant attack from Lord Sydney and some Christchurch members. Such overt divisions would be unthinkable now but Protestants (or evangelicals) attacking those of a Catholic disposition (derogatorily described as Romanists) was, particularly in this decade, a common activity.

In his impassioned article in the Parish Magazine 'R' had exhorted the people to pray the collect for the Sixteenth Sunday after Trinity (above) and to remember that the real enemies of the Church of England were those who 'robbed her of her Catholicity . . . divested her of her priesthood and altar . . . lowered down her ritual and pared away, under the pretence of simplicity, those externals which are necessary for the reverent ordering of her services . . . and would turn her into a miserable Protestant sect of yesterday'.

Few people would now be enraged by commonplace facts of church life such as lighted candles, a cross on the altar or the wearing of vestments. Anyone who now thought about the matter would wonder why such seemingly marginal Church 'goings-on' should have been headline news. The architects of the Oxford Movement had been wary of excessive developments, for their concern was to stress the Early Fathers and the Apostolic nature of the English Church. The responsibility for ritualistic development is more properly laid at the door of the Ecclesiological Society who, through architecture and ornaments, provided the setting for the growing taste in elaborate services. The present day manifestations of a ritualistic urge, apparently so inoffensive, had to be fought for, and although we earlier saw evidence of local outbreaks of physical violence, for example at St Peter's, London Docks, in the 1850s, the 1870s saw ritualism as a national concern.

It was in the 1830s that innovations in church services had begun to appear and, as a counteraction, the Church Discipline Act had come into being in 1840. Note that it was *Parliamentary* legislation that was introduced. This was to be the main objection to all the methods of effecting discipline: that is, the State rather than the Church decreed ecclesiastical law.

Under the Church Discipline Act, anyone could make a complaint to the Bishop. The complainant did not have to be a churchgoer nor even resident in the parish although, in matters of ritual, it was more plausible when the complainant had a legitimate interest in Church affairs. Complaints could be on any matter although doctrine and ritual predominated. The 1867 complaint about FHM to the Archbishop of Canterbury (FHM's Diocesan Bishop) by Lord Sydney, although not specifically invoking the Church Discipline Act was drawing attention to both doctrinal and ritualistic points.

As a further example (indeed there are many to choose from) 1869 saw yet another accusation against Charles Lowder at St Peter's, London Docks. The Bishop of London, although admiring Lowder's work in the poor East End parish, had been obliged to admonish Lowder on his use of elaborate ritual: this, Lowder maintained, was essential for the type of congregation he served. Like the majority of accused ritualists, he politely ignored the episcopal monitions. The 1869 complaint embraced lighted candles, incense, elevation of cup and paten, genuflecting during the prayer of consecration and carrying lighted candles, cross, crucifix and banners in procession.

In the first instance the Bishop, on receipt of a complaint, could issue a warning. If this proved ineffective the Bishop could go further and send the matter on to the Court of Arches which was in a position to suspend or even to deprive the accused of his living.

On the whole, the Church Discipline Act was a failure if success is to be judged by the number of suspensions and deprivations or, more importantly, by the lessening of ritualistic activity. The explanation for the failure lies in the apparently lukewarm response of the Bishops who found themselves in a difficult position if advanced ritual at a particular church seemed to be the will of the congregation. The last thing a bishop wanted was an uproar in his diocese; a monition could be effected by post or by personal interview and as such it remained a quiet matter between a few people (see Chapter10 for the Lord Sydney complaint against FHM in 1867). Without exception the accused clergymen were hard working and sincere and Bishops wanted to retain such men – if only they would toe the line. To send the matter on to the Court of Arches was to open it out to public view and to make a scandal of it. Cases did go to the Court of Arches but compared with the number of complaints they were few.

* * *

But there was another reason for the low key approach of most bishops. In 1865 the Church Association[1] had been formed: this was a Protestant organisation created '...to counteract the efforts now being made to pervert the teaching of the Church of England . . . and to assimilate her services to those of the Church of Rome'. Its methods were manipulative and bishops were, frankly, being disagreeably pressured: very few bishops could be said to have been helpful. The Church Association lagged five years behind the English Church Union (ECU)[2] whose object was 'to defend and further the spread of High Church principles in the Church of England'. As far as membership went the two organisations were more or less equal except that the English Church Union was largely clerical whereas the Church Association was composed mostly of the laity. This polarisation hints that ritualism was provoking a streak of anti-clericalism in Britain, probably fuelled by the colourful and radical style of many of the ritualists. After the somnolence of the eighteenth and the start of the nineteenth century, clergy were now realising their true vocation and were no longer quietly fitting into the traditional system. As an example, FHM's failure to kow-tow to Lord Sydney was cited by Lord Richard Cavendish as the root cause of Lord Sydney's dissatisfaction.

The Church Association was strongly supported by Parliamentarians of both Houses and gained its impetus from its intention to initiate prosecutions of ritualistic clergy. Meanwhile, the English Church Union, though not entirely a defensive organisation, was formed to support clergy under attack. After 1865 the two organisations were locked in battle, each side raising substantial amounts to fund their activities. The Society of the Holy Cross (SSC) made donations to the ECU, for many of their own members were targets. The methods of the Church Association did have an element of conspiracy about them. For example, Fr Alexander Mackonochie, Vicar of St Alban's, Holborn, a leading member of the SSC and friend of Murray and Lowder, was constantly persecuted by the Church Association. Unable to find an 'aggrieved parishioner' to initiate an attack against him, they had to resort to a non-resident who had the dubious qualification of being the secretary of a school in the parish. In the first judgement, several points were decided in favour of Mackonochie and no order was made as to costs. Upon appeal to the Privy Council practically all the points were decided against him and he was ordered to pay all costs, including what the Church Association had spent on hired informers.[3] This was not an isolated instance: the Church Association frequently paid people to attend services with the understanding that they would then file a complaint about what was going on. It is hardly necessary to point out that once the matter had been passed on to the Court of Arches the ritualists themselves did not feel bound to change their ways beyond paying their fines, usually with the help of the ECU. The agitation in the country as a whole reached such a peak that in 1867 a Royal Commission on Ritual was set up.

The Royal Commission took some time to get off the ground as its composition was in itself an added dimension to the controversy. The Marquis of Westmeath presented a petition in the House of Lords with 17,188 Protestant signatures claiming that the conclusions of a Royal Commission on which pro-ritualist bishops sat would be unacceptable. In the event, the pro-ritualists were surprisingly well-represented. Evidence was taken from practising clergy in order to establish the extent of ritualistic activity but more effort was put into deciding the limits of what could be tolerated. The findings of the Royal Commission were hardly conclusive with many of the

Commissioners making their own additional statements. There was no consensus about anti-ritualistic legislation and, when tackled on the subject in 1871 by an impatient Lord Stanhope, the Lord Chancellor stated that not much could be done with such a lack of unanimity on behalf of the Commissioners.

However, the year 1871 might have given some consolation to the Church Association for, as a result of their prosecution of the Rev. John Purchas of St James', Brighton, under the Church Discipline Act, the following were declared illegal: vestments, wafer bread, commixture, and the Eastward position. But it was a hollow victory: the legislation seemed only to strengthen the resolve of the ritualists. For example, in 1869 fourteen London churches had been identified as using vestments but by 1874 that number had risen to thirty. Pusey, a revered figure from the days of the Oxford Movement, determined in 1871, after the Purchas judgement, to adopt the Eastward position when celebrating the Eucharist.

* * *

By May 1873 the Church Association had waited long enough and a memorial carrying the signatures of 60,000 laymen was put before the Archbishops demanding the 'entire suppression of ceremonies and practices adjudged to be illegal'. Tait, no lover of ritual himself but fairminded, described it as 'thirsting for the blood of the ritualists'. There was undoubtedly much exaggeration in the minds of the memorialists who did not recognise that the activities of what was in reality a very small minority of clergy were not going to overthrow the Reformation and surrender the Church of England to Rome. It is also well to remember that most moderate Anglicans had no great enthusiasm for ceremonial but, on the other hand, were not in favour of Parliament restricting the liberty of the Church of England: after all, Parliament was no longer composed exclusively of Anglicans.

A general election took place at the beginning of 1874 and candidates found themselves interrogated by members of the Church Association during the electioneering. There was a change of government and the High Church, pro-ritual Gladstone was ousted by Disraeli who was not minded to resist the pressure for legislation. Indeed, he had the backing of Queen Victoria who had insisted to Archbishop Tait that she wanted something done: she did not like religious extremists. She made her feelings clear when, in 1877, she returned to Charles Lowder a copy of his book *Twenty One Years in St George's Mission.*

After much wrangling, something was done. The Public Worship Regulation Act (PWRA) came into force on 1st July 1875, greeted rapturously by the anti-ritualists in the House of Commons. It was designed to 'facilitate, expedite and cheapen the process' by which clergy guilty of ritual irregularities were disciplined. Lord Shaftesbury was a leading supporter in the Lords and was active in its construction; Gladstone spoke passionately against it; Disraeli, now Prime Minister, gave the Bill his public support. He saw it as an opportunity to 'put down ritualism and destroy the Mass in masquerade'.

The Act was framed to deal with the disobedience which had been a feature of previous attempts at discipline. The ignoring of a judgement was henceforth to be treated as Contempt of Court with the consequent threat of imprisonment. As far as the ritualists were concerned the scene had not changed for the court instituted by the Act was a secular one: the Judge was a layman and Royal Assent was required for the Archbishops' nomination. Indeed, the Crown could appoint if Archbishops did not. The weak spot in achieving the Act's aims was the fact that bishops could veto complaints at an early stage.[4]

The Church Association set to work immediately and attempted eighteen prosecutions in all, sometimes targeting the same person over and over again. A typical example of what happened when these prosecutions went ahead is that of the Rev. Arthur Tooth of St James', Hatcham. Tooth and FHM were friends, FHM acting as a 'Visitor' of the Orphanage recently founded in Hatcham. Tooth was a member of the SSC. A brief look at Tooth's case illustrates how violent were the anti-ritualistic passions. In March 1876, Tooth heard about impending legal proceedings. He wrote to his Bishop (Rochester) denying the authority of the PWRA and on the 2nd December made a protest from the pulpit about the exercise of secular authority in matters spiritual. At the next service after the declaration from the pulpit, 700 attended the Eucharist and Tooth was helped by clergy from St Alban's, Holborn, and St Peter's, London Docks. However, on Christmas Eve the Bishop sent his own Chaplain to conduct the service. At this, Tooth, with the utmost courtesy, stated his rights as the lawful and canonically instituted incumbent of the parish and refused the Bishop's Chaplain the right to take part in the service – at which the Chaplain withdrew.

The ensuing weeks saw the strangest scenes. 'There began a series of riots organised and paid for by the leaders of the Protestant underworld. Men of the lowest type were paid two shillings or more a Sunday; they came in hundreds. Catholics came too from every part of London, among them the President of the ECU, Lord Halifax. Amid the shouts and hisses of the Protestants the service went on. After the service the vicar had to be conducted to the Vicarage by a body of faithful men.[5] The windows of the church were broken . . . attempts were made to break down the church doors . . . many members of the congregation were assaulted.'[6] The police were unable to keep order.

On 22nd January Tooth was arrested and taken to Horsemonger Lane Gaol. After the stress of the last year and now incarceration, Tooth was broken in health and even his foes requested his release after about a month. He went abroad to recuperate and in the meantime the Archbishop appointed a 'Low Church' clergyman who changed the character of the church entirely: all the ornaments of the church were removed by order of the Chancellor's Court including the cross and candlesticks from the High Altar. Tooth returned in May and, finding his church locked against him, made his entrance by a window, and again celebrated Mass. On his subsequent resignation it was found that in his absence the advowson of his church had been secured privately and handed over to a Protestant trust.

* * *

The extremes of the PWRA did not touch Chislehurst but FHM made a significant stand in the Spring of 1879 when he invited Tooth to give the Lent lectures for the St Nicholas' congregation. It is difficult to understand what his real motive was for he could surely have foreseen that it would be a provoking action. As was to be expected there was a letter of complaint to the Archbishop of Canterbury who declined to reveal the source of his information.[7] Archbishop Tait admonished FHM thus: '. . . I cannot help saying to you that I think it an injudicious step on your part to put him [Tooth] so prominently forward in your church as the instructor of your people seeing that his sole claim to be thus selected rests on the miserable proceedings at Hatcham . . .' Tait appealed to FHM's previously avowed respect for the advice of his Bishop. FHM replied to the Archbishop with a 'butter wouldn't melt in my mouth' tone.[8] He assured Tait that he had not asked Tooth because of his notoriety but because of his experience in delivering Lent addresses. Also, he knew that Tooth was now more free to give of his time as he no longer had parochial duties.

The fact that FHM escaped so lightly in the wake of the PWRA is probably because his churchmanship was but moderately 'high': the Church Association was almost on his doorstep and yet never took action against him. It was on 24th July 1877 that there had been an inaugural meeting of the Chislehurst branch of the Church Association. The attendance was large, under the presidency of the Rev. W. Fleming of Christchurch, and 'the proceedings throughout were marked by enthusiasm and unanimity'.[9] After countering the criticism that the Church Association was 'an attacking and persecuting society' the lecturer thumped home the evils of Romanism to the cheers and applause of the audience. The interesting opinion was put forward that it was England's Protestantism that had enabled her to reach her present high position in the world and that 'wherever Romanism had prevailed, the country under its influence had sunk in the scale of nations'. The aspect of 'Romanism' that attracted most indignation was the matter of Confession. A few days later there was a follow-up meeting in Beckenham where 'the room was crowded and the meeting passed off harmoniously and enthusiastically'. An interesting point from this meeting was that in their drive for members they would admit working men at a reduced fee!

* * *

The PWRA was of real concern to the SSC whose members were anxious but determined. Their May Synod of 1875 was largely devoted to the preparation of agreed strategies and FHM, as one of the 'elder Incumbents among the Brethren', was deputed to deliver a paper on the subject of the PWRA. With due modesty as to his non-legal background FHM proposed to discuss 'the general principles affecting its authority' and how binding it was on the clergy. He started: 'Being the law of the land we are necessarily subject to the stringent provisions of it'. He continued: 'In considering the authority of the Act a line may be taken that it is one enforced upon the Church by Act of Parliament alone without any real consent, indeed, against the protest of the Lower House of Convocation, and so it is not binding upon the conscience of any Incumbent; and it may be considered that any Bishop acting upon its provisions is simply doing so to carry out a law of Parliament – acting as a *State Officer*, rather than in his spiritual capacity as a Bishop'. He went on to say that it would seem that, because of the power of the law, a resister would now be obliged to succumb or be deprived. Probably recalling his tactics when faced with Lord Sydney's attacks, he advised that as soon as a complaint was suspected the best course was 'to endeavour to deal with the Bishop in the *spiritual capacity* . . . in which, irrespective of the Act, we may appeal'. He believed that most Bishops would surely try to carry out the Act with consideration: 'The great power of absolute veto will rest with them. . . . Further they have the power of interfering with and staying entirely the execution of the law by *barring any further proceeding* . . . I think *the most should be made of* this great power of arbitration and conciliation'.

FHM advised the earliest possible approach to a Bishop and trusted that most Bishops would wish to be brought in at an early stage. He felt some pity for Bishops in general who were, according to the Act, facing a simplified procedure, but 'will be pestered with trivial cases which they will think should not go forward and yet will find it hard to satisfy the objection of the Protestant world . . . Most of the Bishops will be glad to pacify if possible – to get rid of cases, to deal softly with them rather than to allow them to pass on to the Judge'. However, FHM could see that a difficulty here was that, by the Act, a Bishop had to state his reasons in writing and deposit the document in the Registry of the Diocese. Nevertheless, there was a small loophole in that the Act did not state the time limit that must be observed before the statement need be filed.

FHM's approach was dependent upon amicable relationships with Bishops and he foresaw that many anomalies were likely to arise because of their differing attitudes. His conclusion was that, should a bishop decide not to deal with the matter himself but to submit it to the Archbishop of the province (only an Archbishop had the power to require the services of a Judge) then he could not see how the accused member of the clergy could continue to resist without becoming a law-breaker. This was a serious matter for the Brethren to discuss. Could they, either overtly or covertly, encourage their members to break the law?

On the other hand, he added, 'I do not see how we can, as priests, submit to plead before a court which is constituted simply by an Act of Parliament . . . a court which has no ecclesiastical sanction or character . . . I think the answer is emphatically in the negative'.

FHM's speech ended in challenging style. 'We have no time to lose before the hour comes when the knock may come at our own door, and "*Proximus ardet Ucalegon*"[10] sounds in our waking ears . . . I hope that a conciliatory and dutiful course of reference to the Bishop in his spiritual capacity . . . may be followed . . . For it must be remembered that, let monitions once be issued, then the penalties to which Incumbents are liable for disobedience culminate quickly, in three years, in deprivation . . .'

'If such disobedience is necessary on *principle*, and we are called to suffer *for principle* and for conscience sake, for what we believe to be the law and standard of the Catholic Church, and of the Catholic usage of the Church of England, then the law of suffering for conscience sake will bring its blessing, and the blood of suffering triumph in the eventual promotion of truth.'

Although the PWRA threatened members of the SSC it must be remembered that the SSC was a 'secret' society and opposition to the Bill was evident beyond its membership, even before it became law. There had been 211 petitions *in favour* of the Public Worship Regulation Bill, signed in all by 2,392 persons, and 625 petitions *against* the Bill signed by a total of 20,949 persons. In July 1874 a petition had been organised in Chislehurst and communicants were asked to put their signatures to a document requesting that the Bill should be rejected: 'Your parishioners believe that this Bill, if carried into law, will open the way for vexatious litigation in every parish, will greatly disturb the peace of the Church and instead of composing will embitter existing differences'.

Once the Act was passed there were just eight cases where prosecution ran its full course, two of them were brought under the provisions of the Church Discipline Act of 1840. All of the threatened clergy lived lives of punishing asceticism but the toll in broken health due to this and the strain of constant attack should have been a scandal. Five clergy suffered imprisonment. They were: Arthur Tooth of Hatcham, Thomas Pelham Dale of St Vedast's in the City of London, R.W. Enraght of Birmingham, S.F. Green of Manchester and Bell Cox of Liverpool. On the whole the length of time in gaol was a matter of weeks but Green suffered for eighteen months.

It may seem unexpected that Charles Lowder should not be in the list of prosecutions: he had been protected by the Bishop's veto. The Church Association's fury at the half-hearted response of the Bishops led to further developments which go beyond the scope of this book. A full account of the whole business can be found in Nigel Yates' *Anglican Ritualism in Victorian Britain.*

Those who suffered imprisonment are evidence that FHM was accurately expressing the mind of the SSC in his paper on the PWRA. However, the next test came, unexpectedly, from quite a different source and resulted in the near downfall of the SSC.

* * *

Although FHM has been described as a High Churchman it could not have been said at this time, nor at any other time, that St Nicholas' Church was in the same class as St Peter's, London Docks, the notorious St Alban's, Holborn, nor St Saviour's, Leeds. FHM warned his parishioners of any innovations and endeavoured to bring them along with him backing up his intentions with justification from the Bible or the Prayer Book. He was willing to wait if he felt that he was pushing the congregation too far. When the Church of the Annunciation was built, he ensured that the ceremonial (which he would doubtless have liked at St Nicholas') could flourish in the new setting. In Chapter 11 we saw how he guaranteed that it should remain that way. FHM was not the only pioneering ritualist to use the device of appointing Keble College as patrons of the living of a new church: the same was true of St Barnabas', Tunbridge Wells.

After his arrival in 1846, FHM had gradually increased the number of church services, a sure indication of his overall intentions, and by 1864 there were daily services in the church. In 1872 the daily celebration of the Eucharist was established, inspired by experiences in the Austrian Tyrol in 1871: 'On returning home, I preached four sermons on the subject, bringing it clearly and definitely before the congregation. I did not at once propose such an important change, but I asked them to make it the subject of prayer for guidance.'

Meanwhile, an impressive stock of ornaments and vestments was being accumulated at St Nicholas' and an inventory of 1887 survives. This lists more than one hundred items: chalice and patens as would be expected, together with candlesticks, altar fabrics, vestments, etc. Had all the candles been lighted, as they were at major festivals, there would have been forty lighted candles on the altar, a further twenty elsewhere in the sanctuary and even fourteen on the top of the chancel screen.[11] By 1902, the year of FHM's death, at least another fifty items had appeared on the list.

---

1 This organisation is now known as The Church Society.

2 The parish of St Nicholas' supported the ECU. They frequently invited representative speakers and ECU articles were published in the Parish Magazine.

3 In January 1869 a monition directed him to obey the judgement but by December of that year he had shown no sign of responding. In November 1870 a further judgement was given against him and he was suspended for three months. Further prosecutions followed in 1874 and 1882. Finally, in 1882 he resigned the living of St Alban's, Holborn, and became Vicar of St Peter's, London Docks. However, with the threat of further litigation he resigned and returned to Holborn where he worked unofficially for the rest of his life. The litigation, although punishing to his career and health, had the effect of showing the necessity of settling Church law. In poor health and becoming confused, he died in 1887 while out walking in Scotland. He was aged 62.

4 This advantage was largely due to the intervention of Gladstone.

5 'Heavies' brought in from the congregation of St Peter's, London Docks.

6 From the pamphlet series entitled, *Heroes of the Catholic Revival.*

7 In fact, it was Lord Sydney. He ended his letter to the Archbishop with the question 'What is going on at the Parish Church of Chislehurst?'

8 FHM did indeed have a smooth and ingratiating way with a letter. However, when criticised anonymously in 1873 about the circulation of a book, he firmly wrote to the Archbishop that he 'would not defend himself against anonymous complaints'.

9 All references to the meeting are taken from the account in the August edition of *The Bromley Record*, 1877.

10 *Aeneid* II. 311f.

11 These details are taken from Nigel Yates, *Kent and the Oxford Movement.*

Chapter 14

Societas Sanctae Crucis
(part two)
The Priest in Absolution

The controversy over private Confession is a valuable sidelight on the social attitudes of the late Victorian period and the potential conflict between social stability and spiritual perfection.

NIGEL YATES, *Jesuits in Disguise?*

The beginning of May 1873 was a busy time. It was on 5th May that the petition of 60,000 names was delivered to the two Archbishops. With so many petitions circulating it would be easy to forget which was which. This one was organised by an increasingly militant Church Association, angry at the Bishops' dilatoriness, and exhorting them to enforce the law. It was the petition which provoked from Tait the memorable words, 'thirsting for the blood of the ritualists'(Chapter 13).

On 9th May there arrived, for the attention of the Upper House of Convocation, a petition from 483 clergymen which almost made the Bishops think again. Tait set the mood by attacking it with a sarcastic and disparaging condemnation. This petition had been organised by Lowder – although only 123 signatures were those of SSC members – and it had been in the pipeline for some time. As Victorian petitions went it was quite modest in the numbers it represented: there would have been more signatures had leading figures such as Pusey and Liddon[1] put their names to it.

From the minutes of the SSC it is clear that FHM was party to the framing of the document which was finalised at the March meeting of the Chapter. Briefly, the contents of the petition were as follows: that there should be certain revisions to the Book of Common Prayer based on the First Book of Common Prayer of Edward VI;[2] that more Feast Days should be incorporated into the Church's calendar; that there should be provision for Communion at Marriages and Burials; that provision should be made for the reverent Reservation of the Blessed Eucharist and an Office be prepared for the Communion of the Sick; also a service for the Consecration of Churches and Cemeteries. There was a request for the authorisation of services for Harvest Festivals, the Purification of the Blessed Virgin Mary, Ash Wednesday, Palm Sunday, the last three days of Holy Week and Rogation Days.

The whole petition was rejected but not before an escalation of Episcopal wrath caused by the penultimate section. This read: 'In view of the widespread and increasing use of Sacramental Confession, your venerable House may consider the advisability of providing for the education, selection and licensing of duly qualified confessors, in accordance with the provisions of canon law'. Viewed dispassionately, this was a reasonable request, but as the Bishops perceived no need for Confession nor confessors they were hardly likely to admit that any training was needed. Sidestepping the request, they put their minds instead to the urgent abolition of the use of the Confessional: a committee was formed for the eradication of the evil. In July of that year the Bishops produced their own statement on Confession (end of Chapter 10).

The idea of Confession was guaranteed to bring about a near-hysterical response but it was indeed a growing practice. The Bishops rejected it on an orthodox interpretation of the Prayer Book. Protestants saw it as a denial of their basic belief that the saving death of Jesus Christ gave each believer direct access to God's forgiveness without the need for an intermediary. 'The reserved Anglo-Saxon race was being trained to endure the pain of Confession and to believe that man's "I absolve thee" was the voice of God.'[3] Lord Shaftesbury was furious that the Bishops were entertaining the idea even so far as to discuss the matter. The majority of the public, whether informed or not on religious ideas, loathed Confession as being alien to the English character: it spoke clearly of Popery and devious, manipulating priests. Embry[4] summed up the response: 'The sirens of an anti-confessional agitation were shrieked throughout the country by Protestant associations, and foghorns were sounded by many who lacked experience in penance'.

Absolution is the formal act of a bishop or priest pronouncing the forgiveness of sins by Christ to penitent sinners: the justification is from John 20.21-23. Christ is with his disciples: 'Jesus said to them again, "Peace be with you. As the Father has sent me, even so I send you". And when he had said this, he breathed on them, and said to them, "Receive the Holy Spirit. If you forgive the sins of any, they are forgiven; if you retain the sins of any, they are retained"'.

Objections were not aimed at the familiar General Confession followed by one of the forms of absolution: they were aimed at private auricular confession in the presence of a priest who claimed authority to forgive the penitent in God's name. Private and frequent confession had been a medieval development but had no place in the Prayer Book after 1549 except in the Order for the Visitation of the Sick. The rubric says: 'Here shall the sick person be moved to make a special Confession of his sins, if he feel his conscience troubled by any weighty matter. After which Confession, the Priest shall absolve him (if he humbly and heartily desire it) after this sort. *Our Lord Jesus Christ, who hath left power to his Church to absolve all sinners who truly repent and believe in him, of his great mercy forgive thee thine offences: And by his authority committed to me, I absolve thee from all thy sins, In the Name of the Father, and of the Son, and of the Holy Ghost. Amen.*' It was this one particular Confession and Absolution that was allowed by the Bishops in their statement issued on 23rd July 1873.

* * *

After Convocation's rebuttal the problem for the SSC was how to go forward without appearing pugnacious. Four leading members of the SSC, including Pusey and Liddon (who had not signed the original petition), produced a scholarly statement of the position of the Church of England on the matter of Confession. They made the unarguable point that 'if a thing is good for the soul, it ought not to be put off to a possible sick-bed'. With the addition of the signatures of twenty nine moderate clergy (only one ritualist amongst them) the document was printed in *The Times* of 6th December 1873. The SSC felt confident that this piece would 'do its own work' with the public at large.

Lowder published an open letter to John Jackson, Bishop of London, stressing from the point of view of a parish priest the pastoral value of Confession. He argued against the criticism that Confession encouraged morbidity and unmanliness. He pointed out that taking steps to seek out a priest for Confession took courage and was a sign of the penitent's concern over small lapses as well as for exceptional sins. He countered the criticisms that Confession was intrusive in family life and that young people were in danger of gaining undesirable knowledge as a result of a priest's interrogation. He also defended the private nature of Confession: it was not a furtive act but, in the then climate of opinion, it was necessary to be discreet. He challenged the Bishop to investigate the 'extent of Christian spirituality in those parishes where Confession was regularly used'. Despite the opposition to their petition of 1873 the SSC clergy, and many others, continued to provide for Confession. They were confident that the practice was so widespread that it could not now be eradicated.

By hearing Confessions the members of the SSC believed that they were making the Church more responsive to the needs of devout congregations but there was a suspicion, even amongst some brethren, that the emphasis was getting out of hand, appearing almost fanatical. There is evidence, both before and after 1873, that FHM favoured the spread of Confession but in a restrained way. The SSC minutes are one source of evidence. He had been active in discussions since 1857 and was in charge of the planning of the Cuddesdon Retreat of 1858 at which Richard Meux Benson, the conductor, encouraged Confession and suggested that the brethren should hear each other. In 1859 Brother Littledale drew attention to the want of a Manual of Confession for English priests: the Master noted that this had been under consideration for some time and that he was intending to hold monthly clerical meetings for training. In 1858 it had been recorded that the SSC desired to present an 'Address to Convocation on Confession' but had held back, hoping that the time would be right at some later date. As it turned out, they included the matter in the petition to Convocation of 1873 which, judging from the reaction of the Bishops, was clearly *not* the right time.

* * *

We move on now to 1877. On 20th June, FHM arrived home from the Holy Land to find that Lowder had come over to Chislehurst to meet him: this was probably to prepare him for the letter which had arrived from the Archbishop of Canterbury. 'My attention has been drawn to the book, *The Priest in Absolution*, some parts of which, it is alleged, are of the most disgusting character. Your name is associated with this book as one of the office bearers of the society from which it is said to emanate. I know your character too well to believe that you would be wittingly mixed up with the matter in question and I shall be glad of any explanation which will enable me to defend you from the aspersion not unnaturally cast on all who are in any way connected with the book.'

FHM replied immediately. He requested an interview for the following day. In his absence abroad there had been released a 'pandemonium of religious frenzy' – but for Lowder's explanation he would have been entirely ignorant of the cause. At the June Chapter of the SSC a matter had been brought to the notice of the brethren (it was not on the agenda): it was to the effect that Lord Redesdale intended to bring the book *The Priest in Absolution* and its connection with the Society in front of the House of Lords. Furthermore the names of all members of the SSC had now been published for all to see – in *The Rock*, an ultra-Protestant weekly paper.

An explanation of the nature of this controversial book, *The Priest in Absolution*, and how it came to be in the possession of the SSC is necessary before one can understand why it should have leapt on to the agenda of such a body as the House of Lords and why FHM should claim ignorance of its existence. It is also necessary to slide back more than a century to a pre-Freudian society which was much obsessed with the veneer of respectability and which displayed disgust, if not disbelief, at those intimate aspects of life which are now common currency in the media.

The Rev. F.L. Bagshawe, Master of the SSC at the time, was asked to describe the genesis of the book to Tait, the Archbishop of Canterbury, in the company of seven of the leading brethren of the SSC who had been summoned to Addington Palace. The date of the meeting was 26th June 1877. It is interesting that the Archbishop gave FHM the burden of organising the deputation of members to speak with him. By this time the Society officers had been requested to hand in to the Archbishop the rules of the SSC, the list of members, and the remaining copies of the offending book. There was anxious hesitation over submitting the rules and the list of members without consultation and also a reluctance to hand over the work of one of their own members, possibly for destruction. However, all requests were complied with.

Bagshawe explained that Confession, as the Archbishop well knew, was an established practice and that many priests had cried out for guidance when faced with the multitude of incidents brought to their notice. After much discussion of the topic within the SSC, one of the members, the Rev. J.C. Chambers was asked to build on the joint deliberations and to provide for this need. He was greatly experienced and had the confidence of all types of people, from Lords and MPs to costermongers. The project, consisting of two volumes, was thereafter the responsibility of Chambers. The first part (1866) was not of too controversial a nature and escaped notice. *The Priest in Absolution: Part II* (1870) was the volume which caused the uproar. Chambers had died in 1874 and his executors had asked the SSC to purchase the remaining copies – or they would be sold. The SSC never advertised the book and great care was taken not to let it fall into the hands of those who wanted it for prurient or polemical reasons. It was admitted that the SSC had never been required to look over the book for revision or editing. However, they did buy the copyright feeling it desirable to keep it from the Book Trade. It was stressed that the book was not sold but *given* to priests who genuinely needed it in their work.

For modern readers who wonder how one small book could cause so much interest it is necessary to know what form it took. It detailed all those sins that might possibly trouble penitents and suggested lists of questions that the priest might ask in order to help the penitent to confess in full, perhaps helping him or her to use the terminology that would clarify the full extent of the sin. How could a priest absolve a penitent if he did not know what was being confessed? Whenever there had previously been scandals about Confession it was always allegations about the questioning of penitents which formed the basis of complaints. A particular danger area was the questioning of young women. For example, way back in 1850, it was alleged that a married woman in Leeds had been asked whether she had had any indecent connection with either her husband or other young men before her marriage.[5] There were many examples of this nature. The SSC themselves had foreseen this and had advised that 'there should be some fixed place for hearing confessions, especially those of women.' There was always the suspicion in the minds of lay people that the confessional could be a convenient opportunity for a sort of voyeurism. The fact that many of the priests who practised Confession were unmarried was a troublesome thought.

Much space in the book was devoted to impure thoughts and 'dirty actions' and habits which were usually reckoned to be unmentionable. Children also were seen to be at risk in the close and squalid conditions of the slums and similarly, as a correspondent to the Archbishop pointed out, those in Public Schools and the Services. The book was so outspoken as to prompt from one critic the suggestion that, had it been veiled in Latin, it could perhaps have been tolerated.

* * *

As Tait was dealing with the SSC deputation the matter was making its debut in the House of Lords: in spite of the SSC's security the book had somehow fallen into the hands of Lord Redesdale who, although a moderate man, fulminated with passion against its content and against the sinister organisation which had originally commissioned it. He conceded that 'one or two' members of the SSC did not know of the existence of the book but that the majority distinctly endorsed it and denounced the criticisms. Lord Redesdale's speech which filled a complete column of *The Times* ended with: 'Every clergyman who continues a member of the Society must from henceforth be regarded as a pledged representative of a system utterly abhorrent from the teaching of the Church of England and demoralising to the men, women and children of the nation'.

A fortnight later *The Times* devoted a further two columns to the matter when it reported the debate in the House of Commons. 'The case is not merely that of one or two fanatics circulating doctrines which, at any rate in England, are not likely to find many adherents, but of an association of clergymen of a great national institution, organising a kind of conspiracy for the stealthy introduction of practices which this nation regards as detestable, and for that purpose circulating among themselves a secret manual of a character which at once explains and justifies such detestation.'

The Archbishop's postbag contained many letters from the public, not all of them deploring the book or the SSC. One correspondent, Henry Neville, made a reasoned defence of the book: 'They may be indelicate questions but what about indelicate sins?

Would the same questions from a doctor be so bad?' (This point was also raised in a supportive letter to *The Times*.)

There were letters from women, mostly with fashionable addresses, who were appalled at the suggestion that they would submit to the kind of questioning being exposed. Their use of the Confessional over many years was now causing them unjustified embarrassment.

The Chaplain of the Middlesex House of Correction wrote of the 'awful prevalence of all forms of impurity and bestiality'. As a Chaplain he was obliged to plunge even deeper into the mire than an ordinary parish priest and he described the dreadful abuse suffered by children in overcrowded conditions and the damage to their growing minds of sexual knowledge at too early an age. He implored the Archbishop to 'affirm the necessity of this book'.

Members of the SSC wrote of how the Society had helped them to raise their standard of daily life with untold spiritual benefits. Bishop Jenner felt that the outcry was unreasonable and he would *not* sever his connection: nevertheless, he thought that the remaining copies of the book should be destroyed.

Reading the accounts in *The Times* it is obvious that no one was going to publicise the real values of the SSC. The position of parish priests who had been named in *The Rock* was precarious and that of unbeneficed priests was critical, for the only three Bishops willing to license members of the SSC were Winchester, Oxford and Worcester. The Archbishop of Canterbury thought that there would be so many resignations that the Society would be dissolved: '... I shall be truly glad to find that an organisation which is so much disapproved of by the Heads of the Church ceases to exist.'[6]

* * *

On the first possible Sunday, 24th July, FHM stood in his pulpit to make a statement to his congregation. He sent a copy to the Archbishop. 'As I am not able to speak to you at another time this morning I wish to avail myself for a few moments of this opportunity of addressing you. First, some loving words of greeting on being blessed again to be amongst you . . . But I must deeply regret that this great pleasure has been mixed with a most unexpected trouble which has caused us great distress and anxiety and has given me a week of pain. A society which has nobly served the Church and to which I have belonged for more than twenty years has been lately charged with indiscretion as to a certain book. In common with other friends . . . I feel the strongest possible objection to certain portions of the book which have now been publicly referred to. With regard to this I had an interview by appointment with the Archbishop. No one could possibly be kinder or more considerate than His Grace was to me . . . there are some further points which have deeply affected the public mind upon which I cannot enter here but I shall be glad to give any explanation to anyone who will speak to me, and also to attend any private meeting of gentlemen representative of this congregation and of the Church of the Annunciation who may desire it at any time. I hope, please God, that this will tend to dispel and quiet the serious difficulties which have been felt and with which I most fully sympathise.

'For my own part and for the clergy with whom I have been associated I say to you, my dear friends and parishioners, that I could not stand here for a moment if I felt in the least degree that I or they had done anything which was not becoming to the character of a clergyman and high-minded gentleman.

'I most earnestly trust that when all is understood and calmly considered, when the true facts are fully known, nothing will disturb that loving confidence on your part for which I hope a life and character of thirty years amongst you may be some justification: which confidence is as dear to me as my own honour and without which I could not possibly hold my position among you.'

To his Churchwarden, Mr Janson, he wrote that he could now say what he could not say in church: 'that I wish entirely to disown the book in question. As a matter of fact I had never really read or used it. Having seen more of it, it appears to contain much useful and carefully prepared matter but I disapprove so much of the general line which it follows and so entirely object to certain portions that I wish to separate myself altogether from it . . . please take no action yet.'

On 30th June there is a letter from Bagshawe to the Archbishop. 'Mr Murray and some others have always disapproved of the word Mass. He has always I believe considered that the Society did real good in helping clergy, especially in the country, to keep up a high tone in their religious life and he has therefore never left us.'

The letter from the Archbishop to FHM, on receipt of the pulpit declaration and the letter to Mr Janson, went: 'It has been a great satisfaction to me to receive the papers you have sent and I await further communications'.

On 5th July Mr Janson and the other Churchwarden, Mr Charrington, sent to the Archbishop a very stylish printed document in perfect copperplate: 'We the undersigned, being heads of families and members of the congregation attending St Nicholas' Church, Chislehurst, having considered the statement of Mr Murray read by him in church . . . desire to express the relief in anxiety which they experience in learning that Mr Murray wishes to "entirely disown" and to "separate himself altogether" from the book in question while it would afford them much additional gratification to find that Mr Murray had withdrawn from the above-named Society.

'Further, having regard to the declaration appended here [the Bishops' Report on Confession], the undersigned would most respectfully but earnestly urge Mr Murray unreservedly to accept such declaration, and not by himself or his Curates to enjoin or even encourage any practice of habitual Confession for a priest.'

In a letter to the Archbishop's Chaplain, dated 11th July, Charrington states: '. . . that as Mr Murray has withdrawn from the Society of the Holy Cross there will be no further need to trouble the Archbishop of Canterbury.'

* * *

So ended FHM's involvement with the SSC and with that, the withdrawal from the national stage of Church life. There was just a short time in 1892, at the age of seventy two, when he became a member of Convocation.

He remained convinced of the value of Confession. In 1884, he wrote a preface to

Pusey's pamphlet *Hints for a first Confession* but a surviving letter of that year to Wainwright, the new vicar of St Peter's, London Docks, provides evidence, yet again, of his caution. 'I saw in *The Times* that the Church Association, calling the Bishop's attention to your appointment, has mentioned that in the church are placed not only places for confession *but also* words for the use of penitents. "I confess to God almighty, to Blessed Mary and all the Saints etc." are put in the church. I know such words occur in the *Vade Mecum* – I always scratch them out if I find anyone having the book and so using it . . . it is most unwise to put them up in the church . . . these kinds of things will kill us. I am sure many persons will feel *very strongly* about this as I do myself. You will excuse my writing to urge this. *It is most* important.'

As for the SSC, it did not die: it continues to this day. However, Bagshawe and Lowder, to name but two, suffered stress over *The Priest in Absolution* affair and their failing health and early deaths can probably be attributed in part to the prolonged attack on the SSC.

The minutes of 11th December, no FHM present, contain Brother Bryan King's suggestion that at the present time and in the present circumstances, brethren might withdraw from the Society with the understanding that at some future time they might have their names replaced on the roll. One member maintained that this was tantamount to denial of the faith but it was generally agreed that there should be no imputation of motives to those who thought fit to withdraw from the Society. In fact the number of SSC casualties amounted to 170 over two years: the membership fell from 397 to 227.

It had been a testing time and the result was, in truth, inconclusive. When the *furore* had died down all continued as before. Confession continued to attract more penitents but it remained a target for those who saw ritualists as double-dealers who claimed to be Anglican but who were, in effect, doing the work of Rome. According to Embry[7] there was at least one redeeming point: 'Of those who were chiefly concerned, there was on either side no rancour. The Archbishop used words of unmistakable condemnation which, considering his religious prejudices were not surprising, but he uttered them as gently as possible . . . On the side of SSC no single word of bitterness was used in its deliberations.'

---

1 Henry Parry Liddon was made a Canon of St Paul's Cathedral in 1870. He was the first Vice-Principal of Cuddesdon Theological College and then Vice-Principal of St Edmund Hall, Oxford. These are but three of his many senior positions in the Church. He exerted a vast influence over post-Tractarian developments and devoted the last years of his life to a biography of Pusey.

2 The most Catholic version.

3 From the speech at the formation of the Chislehurst Branch of the Church Association.

4 J. Embry, *The Catholic Movement and SSC.*

5 Incident related by Nigel Yates, Journal of Ecclesiastical History, Vol. 39, No. 2, *'Jesuits in Disguise?'*

6 Letter to T.T. Carter, a member of SSC, Rector of Clewer near Windsor and founder, at Clewer, of the House of Mercy for the rescue of fallen women; also a sisterhood, The Community of St John the Baptist.

7 J Embry, *op. cit.*

Chapter 15

The Death of Lowder

To the burial here of non-parishioners we owe the possession of the tomb of the Rev. Father Lowder, which in itself makes the Chislehurst churchyard a place of interest . . . the anniversary of his death brings many of his old parishioners from St Peter's, London Docks, to visit the grave. The beautiful marble cross is on the north side of the church and stands a little higher than those around it.

WEBB, MILLER and BECKWITH, *The History of Chislehurst.*

The 1870s was a decade of stress in the Church both for ritualists and no doubt for their antagonists as well. A leading ritualist figure like Lowder found himself in demand on a variety of platforms, not only as an officer of his own organisation, the SSC, with which he had been deeply involved since 1855, but also as a committee member for organisations such as the English Church Union and the Confraternity of the Blessed Sacrament.

At the beginning of 1870 there was but one Curate to help him at St Peter's. In 1868 he had suffered a blow when three of his Curates went over to Rome, lacking the courage to discuss this with him. Their secessions called up another phase of persecution from the Church Association. In the Curates' defence, the apparent cowardice may have been a result of Lowder's austere manner which made him unapproachable, even seemingly unkind in his dealings with his colleagues. He was economical in praising his young clergy. The people of the parish, who 'respected and admired him could not all at once get at his heart'.[1]

In her book, *Charles Lowder and the Ritualist Movement*, L.E. Ellsworth spells out the kind of programme he maintained during the latter part of 1870. 'On Wednesday 22nd June, Lowder had turned fifty. Having said Mass at St Peter's, he departed "for a day of fresh air" at Chislehurst from which he returned on the following evening to prepare for the festival on the 29th.' For a month after that Lowder was solely in charge of the parish while the Curate was on holiday. Lowder himself then took a sightseeing holiday in Wales leaving his Curate on duty. In September he attended the Southampton Church Congress. In November he spent eleven days in Devon when, with other SSC members, he organised and conducted a mission for five churches in Plymouth and Devonport. The mission was a success but Lowder returned to Wapping suffering from food poisoning and a subsequent exhaustion. The time had now come to make preparations for Advent and Christmas. During Advent both of his parents became ill and as Lowder vested for the 6am Eucharist on Christmas Day he was summoned home to his mother's deathbed. Her death, ten days later, had a profound effect on him and many noted that he was thereafter a changed man: compassion became his mark and with the daily visiting of homes, sharing the concerns of the people, he gradually drew their love to himself.

Although Lowder gave himself a heavy programme outside Wapping the intensity and strain of parish life must not be underestimated. Day to day work was long and arduous. We owe a description of daily life at St Peter's to a later curate, Fr Linklater. Services on every day of the week started at 7am if not earlier, so that the labouring men could attend, and there would be no breakfast for the clergy until after 9am: this would be a frugal affair in the Clergy House. On a Sunday, there would be Mattins at 10.15am followed at 11am by the High Celebration of Mass. An hour would be allowed for dinner but before it was over the clergy would be interrupted by the noise of the arrival of the 'big lads' for their Sunday Class. At 3.30pm there would be 'catechising' followed by 'Guild Meetings'. There was tea at 5.30pm but even there an element of duty was present for the clergy would entertain the choirboys to tea in small groups on a rota basis. At 7pm there was a sung Evensong at which Lowder always preached and this service was sometimes 'literally crammed'. After this service there was often a Bible Class for which the greater part of the congregation stayed behind. The weekday work of the clergy was no less demanding than that of Sundays, rarely finishing before 9pm.

In spite of the severe conditions the problem of keeping clergy melted away after 1871 and thereafter there were never fewer than three curates. Fr Wainwright, who was appointed after lengthy consideration by Lowder, wrote: 'To be on the staff of St Peter's in those days was looked on as a great privilege, so great that I hardly dared to hope that it would fall to my lot'. However, the massive social problems of the area and the density of the vast population required a far greater input than even four clergy could provide. As well as maintaining an active and growing church they were combining the services of the then non-existent Social Services and National Health Service.[2] In addition they were organising, with the Sisters of Mercy, the only education available for both children and adults. They were abundantly innovative (for example, Linklater mentioned a 'stringed band' practice) but were hard put to carry through their many projects.

The Community of the Holy Cross, the Sisterhood which had run the House of Mercy in Wapping from the early days had, because of increasing numbers, been transferred to Walworth leaving behind just three Sisters and an associate. Lowder continued as their Chaplain but he resigned the Visitorship of the Community.

Life in the Clergy House was of a disciplined, monastic style with little time for recreation: any spare time between sick visiting, Bible Classes or teaching in the school was spent in serious reading, or writing sermons and letters. Overhanging all of this was the frustrating shortage of funds and the nagging ill-health caused by the austere life and diet. As has been mentioned, Chislehurst was Lowder's place of relaxation but it must be significant that he endeavoured to escape for his holidays to pure mountain air.

Nothing was easy in the parish. Fr Linklater wrote of the immense effort required to knock on the first door of the day. What response would one receive? With what problems would one be faced? In fact, there soon became no difficulty in obtaining entrance and a new pressure was the desire of the people to see the clergy amongst them. How could just a few clergy satisfy the teeming thousands? The church attendance was high to overflowing but there was always the drive in the clergy mind to move amongst those others, the majority, as yet untouched by the Church. Fr Linklater ran a night school and Bible Class. He said: 'My Bible Class was a surging mob of noisy and blaspheming roughs. We never dared to venture on a prayer and often had to stop the hymn because they were only mocking God'.[3] Such evenings were wearing and could only be tolerated with overwhelming commitment to the cause.

In 1874 Wapping was flooded and the clergy had to take the children home in boats. Lowder was fifty four and prematurely aged by care and ill-health but he led the rescue work. One of the clergy remembered: 'When he had been working up to his knees in water for some hours, carrying the children out of school, we had got him some hot brandy and water; he seemed really annoyed at what he thought was a fuss. But his care for others was as great as his want of care for himself: if he thought any of the clergy of the house were ill, he was always the first to make them rest'.[4]

At this time the Church Association, on the introduction of the Public Worship Regulation Act, attempted to prosecute Lowder. Finding an 'aggrieved parishioner' in Wapping was no easy matter, for anyone who took on the role would find himself in peril of his life. When one of the churchwardens noticed what he knew to be Protestant Association spies sitting in church he whispered suitably threatening words in their ears and they were gone in no time. 'They were glad to get away without broken heads.'[5] On the supportive memorial sent to Lowder there were seventeen hundred names. The fact that not all of those who signed were communicants was a source of joy to Lowder for it was a sign that the work, centred on the church, was touching the lives of many more whom the clergy had probably never seen.

In 1875 his health was so poor that he took a break in Italy over Lent and Easter, only to be summoned home on Easter Day on account of the death of his beloved sister Kate Maria. By May, he was so weak that it was necessary to take a lodging in Chislehurst in an attempt to regain strength. 'For a long time he was so broken in health that it was as much as he could do to drag through the duties of Sunday. During this long period [nine months] he lived at Chislehurst which was of easy access and the fine bracing air suited him.'[6] He commuted to Wapping on Sundays to play his part in the services at St Peter's.

In 1877, there was the scandal of *The Priest in Absolution*. This was an unexpected turn of events and one can only speculate on how traumatic the episode must have been, particularly as he was in such a wretched state of health. One of his Curates summed up his situation as 'overwhelming waves of desertion, treachery, disappointment and rebuke'. As soon as the scandal broke he went over to Chislehurst to meet FHM on his return from the Holy Land.

* * *

Throughout the decade Lowder's health deteriorated, probably through the development of a gastric ulcer. Early in 1874 he wrote to his father: 'I have been very tired and unable to get through more than necessary work'. It is clear that the next few punishing years were going to be a major threat to his condition. In an effort to generate some vitality he would regularly spend one day of each week at Chislehurst as a guest of FHM at the Rectory or, after 1877, in the Clergy House.[7] This, at FHM's expense, had been provided for his Curates who were, seemingly without exception, members of the SSC. Lowder would always be present at Chislehurst's festivals and major events.

Lowder was pulled down yet more by the excessively severe winter of 1878/9 and the subsequent distress suffered by the people of Wapping. Fr Linklater recorded: 'Our people have suffered greatly. It is perfectly heart-rending to hear of so many being without fire or food; poor little children coming to school without food, and coming through the slush or snow with broken boots, or no boots at all'. Kind friends, including the people of Chislehurst, did what they could by sending parcels of food and clothing.

However there was some improvement in Lowder's condition when, during the summer of 1879, he took a house in Chislehurst for two of his sisters and spent two or three days a week with them. This still gave him no real escape from the ritualistic disputes which raged around him and the members of the SSC. He took another break in Wales but any good effect was negated by yet another hard winter, 1879/80, when the Mission was overwhelmed by the necessity of providing food, clothing and fuel. To Lowder fell the burden of writing begging letters.

Nevertheless, the progress at St Peter's was encouraging for in November 1879 they had a visit from a reluctant Bishop of Bedford, William Walsham How. He received such a welcome at a meeting of the working men that he agreed to return for a Confirmation in the next spring: there were seventy six candidates, most of them adults. To have such support from a Bishop was a new experience. At the end of June 1880 Lowder felt able to present quite an optimistic report. Unfortunately, this optimism hid a sad decline in his own condition. Wainwright and Lowder's sisters were well aware that he was failing. He was aged sixty.

* * *

The demands on him grew no less for he was an essential element of everything that happened. For example, on Sunday 1st August, he said Mass at 8am, conducted a Baptism during Mattins and then assisted at the usual High Celebration where the numbers were swelled to overflowing by the presence of officers and provincial delegates of the Church of England Working Men's Society. They had come by steamboat from Blackfriars and had marched through the streets accompanied by the band of the St Peter's CEWMS. After the service there was a ceremony at which Lowder was honoured with the silver badge of the Society as a token of his many acts of kindness. However, the day was not over: in the afternoon Lowder joined the children who went off in nineteen vans to Walthamstow for their annual school excursion. 'After a time spent amusing the children he lay on his back in the grass while they alternately clustered round him and used his prone figure as a high jump. Returning to Wapping, Lowder holding one child on each knee, he and the rest of the party were met by the Mission band, which, having enjoyed the morning's effort and wishing to repeat it, escorted the vans into the parish, where for no apparent reason the streets were thronged with cheering parishioners and the buildings decorated with banners and coloured lights.'[8]

He was up early the next morning for Mass, worked at his desk for a while and then with minimal packing set off for his holiday. The holiday started in the company of his sister Rose and a friend; they travelled together to Konstanz in Switzerland. Here they parted while the ladies went towards Schaffhausen and Lowder tackled some high walking with a guide. They met up again at Oberammergau and attended the Passion Play. By 17th August, Rose and her friend left Lowder and arranged to send on luggage to him: he was then joined by two clerics from England. These three gave themselves a gruelling programme of mountain walking, often getting up before dawn in order to reach some distant target by breakfast, regardless of stormy weather. Into the bargain, Lowder wasted valuable energy in fruitless journeys to find his errant luggage. They found themselves at Zell am Zee and the first worrying sign was Lowder's need to leave the Mass at Zell Parish Church and to spend the rest of the day in the hotel. Two days later he was out walking again and on 30th August he was recovered enough to walk for nine hours in bad weather. For many years Lowder had cherished an ambition to climb the Gross Venediger. The climb involved spending the Tuesday night in a mountain hut at about 9,000 feet and then rising at 2am to climb to the summit at 12,000 feet before sunrise. Rumsey, one of the party, wrote: 'The ascent was in perfect weather; a sharp frost and the snow beautifully hard. And the view from the summit was perfect, the clouds all below in the valleys, but the peaks clear in every direction. We could not stay for more than twenty minutes because of the cold'. After this experience, described by Lowder in his notebook as 'a possession for ever', he was persuaded to spare himself over the next day or two and he went back by coach to Zell am Zee.

On the Monday he asked for a doctor. A further visit on the Wednesday caused more concern to the doctor and Lowder, sensing his serious condition, asked whether there was anyone who could take down a letter for him in English. A fellow guest, a Mr Taylor, immediately offered his services. Lowder dictated: 'My dear Annie, I am sorry to have to write by another hand but I have been laid up for a few days by a severe attack of colic brought on by overstrain in mountaineering, and especially by ascending the Gross Venediger. I have had to call in a doctor but I shall not be able to get home by the time I had hoped . . . Please write to Mr Wainwright and say how it is I shall not be able to get to St Peter's when I expected . . .'

An hour or two later he was noticeably worse and although the doctor tried to be encouraging Lowder was well aware of the approach of death. In the night he dictated his final wishes to Mr Taylor: 'I leave all my books to my brother . . . the little money I have, to my sisters. If in consecrated ground, here I wish to be buried, if not at Chislehurst . . .'

Mr Taylor's daughter spoke German and was called in to act as an interpreter when the local priest arrived but it seems that, even in the extreme circumstances, Lowder's German sufficed. The priest, kind and simple, was doubtful about ministering to a non-Roman Catholic and was only willing to give Lowder conditional absolution. On the priest's departure, Miss Taylor was still present and Lowder said to her: 'You are witness that I die in the Anglican Church'. Miss Taylor comforted him by reading prayers. A nurse had been appointed to watch over him and at about 4.30am she called the Taylors to his bedside: they were with him when he died at 5am.

* * *

The people of Wapping were shocked and bewildered by the news but were immediately concerned that he might be buried in Austria, not England. In case the cost should be a problem the St Peter's Working Men's Society quickly got together £30 which they sent off straight away, with the promise of further funds to meet the expenses of transporting the body.

The body arrived on the morning of Friday 17th September, the day set for the funeral. St Peter's was open all night long and the first of twelve Masses was said at 3.20am. The body was met in Wapping by a procession consisting of the clergy of St Peter's and about eighty more mourners together with the choir, the Sisters and many others. The Working Men's Society placed the coffin on the bier and carried it, draped in white, to the church. The streets were lined with weeping parishioners and those who could found places in the church.

For the funeral proper a special train to Chislehurst had been laid on which transported 800 people. There were many more who could not afford the one shilling fare and who walked to Chislehurst from Wapping forming an immense stream of black figures carrying wreaths of fresh flowers. The seats in St Nicholas' were reserved for the people of Wapping who knew Lowder closely but there were also many people of Chislehurst who wished to be counted with them. The hearse was received at the school where a procession formed and we can imagine the spectacle as the coffin was slowly borne across the Common preceded by the choirs of the two churches and followed by the clergy in cassocks and surplices, the Sisters with white wreaths, the members of the Confraternities, and St Peter's congregation. The Rector met the coffin at the lychgate and while the service went on in the church, thousands stood in silence around the churchyard and on the Common. According to one estimate there were 10,000. There were two hundred clergy present.[9]

The grave was lined with ivy and laurel and the north side of the churchyard soon became a sea of flowers as mourners placed their tributes. For a hundred years there was at the graveside a gathering of people from Wapping on 'Lowder Day', the anniversary of his death, 9th September. Today, members of the SSC gather at Chislehurst for a commemorative Eucharist as close as possible to 'Lowder Day'. As a memorial to Lowder a large sum of money was raised to build a complex of appropriate buildings around St Peter's, including a new Clergy House.

Lowder's life was on a heroic scale. His courageous vision of transforming the lives and winning the souls of the deprived people of Wapping seemed hopeless in the early stages and from the outset the work was fraught with opposition from all quarters. But in the course of realising their vision Lowder and his clergy provided a

Members of the SSC at Lowder's grave. Photograph: Peter Rawlins

template for Anglo-Catholic worship. Their conviction and confidence enabled them to carry others with them. They always claimed that ritual was essential in a parish like St Peter's because the people in their poverty needed the stimulation of an exciting presentation of the Christian faith. However, feelings about this have changed: Nigel Yates[10] believes that this is questionable because, on taking a statistical view, most ritualistic churches flourished in middle class areas. He interprets their success in deprived areas to be a consequence of the charisma of the priests in charge.

As an epilogue it is interesting that the priest in Zell am Zee must have come to realise what a distinguished priest of the Anglican Church had died in his parish for he decided that a local memorial was in order – even going so far as to suggest that Lowder's heart should be buried in the mountains. This request was flatly refused. My guess is that FHM went to Zell am Zee in 1890 for there exists in the archives at St Peter's a dried clover leaf, attached to a note in FHM's handwriting: 'Gathered in the churchyard, Zell am Zee, from the "English Cross", July 1890'.

1 Madge Darby, *The First Hundred Years at St Peter's, London Docks.*

2 Lowder had personally supervised the management of the serious outbreak of cholera in 1868, putting himself at great risk in his close care of the sick and dying.

3 Madge Darby, *op. cit.*

4 Madge Darby, *op.cit.*

5 DNB

6 L.E. Ellsworth, *Charles Lowder and the Ritualist Movement.*

7 The SSC pioneered the 19th century development of the Anglican 'Clergy House', more usually in urban areas, where a team of priests worked and lived together. A set of Clergy House Rules was devised which ensured a peaceful atmosphere and urged a spirit of forebearance. Silence on the staircase and in passages was enjoined – unless courtesy to a visitor demanded quiet speech. Clergy wore cassocks in the Clergy House and addressed each other as Father.

8 L.E. Ellsworth, *op. cit.*

9 James Skinner, *The Literary Churchman and Fortnightly.*

10 Nigel Yates, *Anglican Ritualism in Victorian Britain, 1830-1910.*

Chapter 16

The Parish, the Schools and the Foundation of St Katharine's, Rotherhithe

Its salubrious climate, fine open landscape and picturesque scenery have made Chislehurst one of the most favourite resorts for pleasure parties from London by road or rail; but to the permanent resident it has many additional advantages. House rents are moderate, rates are low, educational facilities are particularly good and the district is within easy reach of London by rail.

Although the neighbourhood preserves a rural character to a great degree, it has nevertheless very considerable resources both in the way of public institutions and business houses, so that residents need not go beyond the village to obtain all the utilities and luxuries of modern life.

In all directions may be seen handsome mansions and villages, with lawns, parks and gardens set off with belts of woodland scenery of unrivalled beauty.

ROCHARD, *A brief look at Bromley, Beckenham and Chislehurst (1893)*

FHM's fifty-six years as Rector of St Nicholas' Church saw the transformation of Chislehurst from a cluster of fewer than 380 houses to a suburban village of more than 1,400 houses. The growth took off around the year 1860, publicised by a volunteer 'sham fight' on the hill between Bickley and Camden Place, an extraordinary device for drawing attention to Chislehurst as a potential residential area. The consequence was indeed the building of many substantial houses in that part of the village, proximity to the station being an attraction. This area was a little removed from the Parish Church and also downhill from it which accounted, in part, for the establishment in 1872 of Christchurch at the centre of the new housing (Chapter 10).

Between 1861 and 1871 Chislehurst's rate of increase of population was 3.4 times the national average and between 1871 and 1881 this figure rose to 4.4.[1] As the marriage rate was low and births exceeded deaths by only a small margin the conclusion has to be that the growth was mostly because of the influx of inhabitants.

It is interesting to note that women outnumbered men throughout the period, probably because of the employment of women as domestic staff. In 1861 there were 1,220 females to 1,067 men and by 1901 the figures were 4,214 to 3,215. The Rector's household demonstrated this well. Taking 1871 as a representative year the household comprised:

Francis Murray
Mary Murray
Henry Murray (son)
Edgar Dumbleton (visitor; 14yrs)
Mary Stanbrook (cook; 24yrs)
Sarah Stanbrook (parlourmaid; 25yrs)
Jane Watson (housemaid; 22yrs)
John Lovel (page; 14yrs)
Mary Mitcham (kitchenmaid; 18yrs)
Susan Bishop (lady's maid; 25yrs)

In 1861 there had been a groom, male, but by 1871 he, or his successor, was probably living out: there was certainly a cottage for him on glebe land by 1876. The Rector kept a pony and trap as did most of the well-to-do: the station was planned with a broad approach and waiting area to accommodate the crush of vehicles fetching and dropping off those using the trains.

The increase in middle and upper class households was responsible for the attendant increase in Prickend of a working class population which served in every capacity to cater for the needs of the big houses. The Church of the Annunciation, which was initially consecrated in 1870 when Prickend numbered about 900, had a parish consisting of about 3,000 by 1901.

For all that Chislehurst was filling up with wealthy residents it was not the healthy spot that it seemed, especially as the century wore on. Using simple averages for age of death is often misleading but the fact that there were many infant deaths has to be taken into account. For example, in September 1868 there were four burials and the ages of the deceased were: 2yrs 9mths, 2yrs 4mths, 4mths, and 34yrs. During FHM's first five years in Chislehurst the average age of death was comparatively high, that is 40 years; in the 1880s it had gone down to 34 years. Worse still, for six continuous years from 1872 the average age of death for the working classes never rose above 20 years. However, in that time the average for the middle classes never fell below 35 years. The fact was that Chislehurst had severe sanitary and drainage problems which were exacerbated by the increase in population. In 1872, according to the Sanitary Committee Minute Book, it was realised that there were many contaminated wells because of their close proximity to cesspools which were seeping into the chalk. The figure given was sixteen contaminated wells out of thirty tested. In 1880 the Medical Officer of Health was advising piped water. That the wells were the source of much ill health and even death was borne out by the fact that in the area where enteric fever broke out during the 1880s, three of the four wells were contaminated. Specimens of the water showed 'suspended matter in abundance'.

The school log book testifies to recurrent outbreaks of disease amongst the children, not necessarily water-borne conditions: the school was frequently closed because of 'epidemics' of measles, mumps, scarlet fever, diphtheria or whooping cough.

* * *

The St Nicholas' Schools (boys and girls were separate) were of particular concern to the Rector: he and Mrs Murray visited regularly. Visitors to the Rectory usually called in at the Schools and there was a succession of Chislehurst young ladies who gave their time to help with needlework or spelling. Certainly from 1883, and until his death, FHM was the active and conscientious chairman of the committee of trustees.[2] This also involved the oversight of the Prickend School for Infants which at this time was sited in St Mary's Hall, the village hall which served the Church of the Annunciation in Prickend.

When the trustees of St Mary's Hall decided that it was no longer appropriate for the school to be accommodated there, FHM's committee had to come up with a plan for a new building: 'the cordial support and co-operation of the school committee would be given to any well-matured scheme'. Lord Sydney was first approached for he owned a well-placed plot of land in Prickend but he declined to sell. He was not alone in seeming uncooperative, for having a school near one's property was not seen as an advantage. Eventually a suitable half acre of ground was purchased and there the school, for mixed Juniors and Infants, was built in 1885 at a cost of £1,500. This money had to be raised by public subscription and, as usual, the Rector headed the list with a generous donation.[3] Unfortunately, the fact that it was a mixed school seems to have been disastrous. Warning signs were the facts that in February 1887 Miss Tilling was given notice to leave in three months' time and in December 1887 it was announced that three more teachers were leaving. The Inspector's Report was damning: 'The organisation of this school would be greatly improved if boys were not admitted. As a girls' school I see no reason why it should not succeed; as a mixed school, admitting boys, I fear it will never rise above a moderate standard of efficiency . . . The staff . . . is inadequate in quality.' At the next trustees' meeting it was proposed that the Prickend School should have its own management committee: after ten months the Vicar of the Annunciation, the Rev. H. Lloyd Russell, was able to report that he had gathered together a distinguished committee.

* * *

FHM, as chairman of the trustees, was concerned about lateness and absenteeism: to solve these problems the committee came up with many ingenious plans. The principal concern over late arrivals was the fact that Scripture was always the first lesson and many pupils missed this important part of the curriculum day after day. Needless to say, they missed not only Scripture but everything else when they did not arrive at all. A sub-committee was formed to look into the irregularity of attendance. They began by assembling the names, addresses and attendances of all children for a six month period in which there was a possible total of 212 attendances per child. The average absence for boys was 55/212 and for girls 65/212. A personal interview was arranged with each family whose child/children were regularly missing. 'Two of Mr Miller's[4] daughters kindly undertook this and, on calling the attention of the parents to absence or unpunctuality, they found in many cases that the parents were ignorant of it – and in others that they had not realized their obligation to send their children by any definite hour. In no single case did the young ladies find that the children had been purposely withheld from religious instruction.'[5]

The unpaid employment of the Misses Miller for this welfare work was only one of the many instances of the philanthropically inclined people of Chislehurst involving themselves with the schools. The upshot of the report from the Misses Miller was that Mr Eggleton,[6] the headmaster, would in future send lists of absentees each week to the Curate who would distribute the names to a team of 'Misses' who would follow them up in their allotted districts. It was resolved also that all parents should receive notice of the official school hours: 9am-12noon and 2pm-4pm. There was some improvement after this but not enough to merit abandoning the campaign. The next move was to send a card regularly to the parents of those children who habitually arrived late showing the exact time of arrival at school.

If there was trouble in enforcing attendance, extracting the payment of subscriptions was even more of a problem. The subscribing sector of the Chislehurst public made generous donations to keep the school going and parents, as their contribution, had to pay a weekly fee of twopence, later increased to threepence. Non-payment by the parents was such an issue that it was resolved that, after a given date, 'no child is to be admitted to the schools without payment'. However, some parents expressed their view on the matter of payment: Mr Herbert, whose child was not making progress, said that it was not worth twopence a week.

It has to be admitted that all was not well at times and after one particularly damning report at the end of 1883 'all the teachers expressed a wish that as often as possible members of the committee should visit the schools and see for themselves the tuition given as it would encourage the teachers and give confidence to the children'.

* * *

In 1891, the year of the Elementary Education Act, the Honorary Secretary of the trustees wrote to all parents explaining that they had decided to accept the Government Grant: from then onwards education for those between the ages of three and fifteen would be entirely without charge. 'The government compels every child to attend school and the compulsory Clause in the Education Act will now be strictly enforced.' The total annual cost of educating each child was £4, of which hitherto the government had contributed about 17/6, the school pence (the parents' contribution) had amounted to about 11/- leaving the rest of the expense, about £2/11/6, to be made up by public subscription. This was of course going to be a saving for the parents but the trustees were quick to suggest worthy ways in which the parents could now use the extra money. Just absorbing it into the housekeeping was not going to show much long-term benefit, nor even putting it into the Shoe and Clothing Clubs. The best idea was to put the money in the Penny Bank on behalf of the child: 'If a child puts in 3d a week from the age of 3 to 14 it will have more than £7 on leaving school. How often it happens that you are in want of a few pounds at that time to apprentice your children, or to fit them out when they go into service! How many children have become labourers instead of mechanics just for want of a little ready money?' There was also a suggestion that parents should authorise the deduction of not less than 2/6 a year from each Penny Bank account as a donation to the school.

Unfortunately the money situation overall developed badly from this point. This was because St Nicholas' had opted to remain as a Voluntary School, rather than a Board School, which meant that local subscriptions were still needed in abundance. Matters were not helped by the fact that FHM forgot to dedicate one of the church collections, as promised, to the cause. A direct appeal was made to the St Nicholas' congregation. It was pointed out that giving voluntarily was cheaper and more comfortable than having the school costs put on the rates at 1/5 in the pound: this was the rate in nearby Lewisham which had opted for a Board School. The argument was a winner with the Chislehurst people who liked to keep the rates down. For a long time they had delayed having street lighting or the watering of the roads in summer because of the charge on the rates, eventually succumbing in 1893 and 1891 respectively.[7] The appeal for subscribers[8] raised more than £190 from more than eighty families, FHM being well in the lead with his donation of £15.

During the 1890s the Reports on the school were sometimes almost too fulsome to be true but the finance continued to be a problem with a deficit reported at the end of each year. In 1899 it was decided that the children of St Michael's Orphanage should be allowed to attend the school on receipt of an annual payment of at least £20 from the Waifs and Strays Society. The teachers seemed to have been delighted with the high standards of behaviour and endeavour demonstrated by the newcomers.

Before leaving the schools, about which much more could be written, it is amusing to look at some of the comments from the Log Book which, because of their concentration on punishments, give the impression that there was daily mayhem. There were frequent complaints about the distractions caused by the Pleasure Parties on the Common: in fact, keeping the children from escaping on to the Common was a continuous battle. Occasionally the Militia exercised there but, certainly on one such occasion, the teachers caved in and gave the children a half day off. In fact the children frequently had days off because of village events like important funerals or even for the wedding of Miss Nussey (one of the school helpers). Those children without a good attendance record were not encouraged to attend on inspection days: this device, however, did not escape the notice of the inspectors.

One's sympathy goes out to the teachers whose methods and attitudes were so unenlightened that there was little to hold the children's attention. They comforted themselves at one time by the knowledge that the children were extremely weak in intellect anyway: 'The Inspector said today and has often said, that Chislehurst children were certainly the dullest children he had heard. This, he declared, was not for want of instruction but a dull, sluggish understanding'.

The schools put the magnifying glass on the disadvantaged of Chislehurst who were frequently and unashamedly described as the 'poor' in the Parish Magazine, in public documents and in private letters. The generosity of the well-to-do is undisputed but Chislehurst, including FHM, cannot be accused of the merest glimmer of any kind of radical outlook: a well-meaning paternalism was in place. The stance was inevitably conservative and included a dutiful attitude towards the 'poor', shored up by FHM's leadership and the example of neighbours. During hard winters there was a Soup Kitchen in Prickend which was organised by the Vicar's wife, a reminder of the immense role taken on by clergy wives at that time, Mrs Murray included.

* * *

Aware of his parishioners' ready conscience, FHM felt confident of their support for a project more demanding than the 1870 foundation of the Church of the Annunciation. There had been correspondence in *The Times* in 1882 about the need for more churches in London, particularly in populous and deprived areas. As a result the Bishop of Rochester had called for the formation of ten new ecclesiastical districts in south London. In a letter to the Parish Magazine of January 1883 FHM put forward his plans for St Nicholas' Church to play a role in this. 'Will our readers . . . be so good as to contribute something for the benefit of thousands whose lot is cast in less pleasant spots than Chislehurst. Annual subscriptions are requested because of the long-term commitment. We need the active sympathy and support of all if the work is to be carried to a successful issue.'

By February 1883 the matter appears to have been decided: 'The district of St Helena Gardens, Rotherhithe . . . has a special interest for us. We pass it constantly on our journeys to and from London and we can see for ourselves the dreary region . . . consisting entirely of cottages inhabited by the wage-earning classes'.[9] This was an over-picturesque description of an area which was every bit as bad as the dockland surrounding Charles Lowder's church in Wapping.

Way back in 1851 at the time of the Religious Census, taken two days before the Population Census, the Methodist Church woke up to the fact that, though founded originally for and by the working classes of a century earlier, it had by now become a middle class organisation, even running to the exclusivity of pew rents. It was acknowledged that the Methodist Church was not active in the worst areas of cities and the Conference of 1854 decided upon 'reviving the Home Missionary spirit of Methodism'. By 1885, in the city areas where the need was greatest they had set about changing their strongholds, the chapels, into outgoing missionary centres and the London Wesleyan Methodist Mission was established.

They had been powerfully persuaded, in 1883, by a significant pamphlet produced by the Rev. Andrew Mearns, Secretary of the Congregational Union, under the moving title *The Bitter Cry of Outcast London*. A house-to-house survey had been carried out in Bermondsey, Ratcliff and Shadwell and had revealed 'the discovery that seething in the very centre of our great cities, concealed by the thinnest crust of civilisation and decency, is a vast mass of moral corruption, of heart-breaking misery and absolute godlessness . . . The gulf has been daily widening which separates the lowest classes of the community from our churches and chapels, and from all decency and civilisation'. The report made harrowing reading.

It did not catch the public's eye until W.T. Stead, the editor of the *Pall Mall Gazette* and also a Congregationalist, pioneered the modern journalistic technique of making a big story out of a piece of news and sustaining it over many weeks. Stead championed the cause with great effect and south London became the target of much energetic missionary activity which included numerous University and Public School settlements. This continued well into the twentieth century and the joke was that there were more missionaries in Bermondsey than in Africa!

* * *

Stead's broadcasting of *The Bitter Cry of Outcast London* and the resulting zeal of the non-conformists must surely have reached the ears of Chislehurst people who were busy playing their part by raising money for the new Church of St Katharine in Rotherhithe. The fact that the report was concerned with areas already familiar to the people of Chislehurst must have strengthened their determination (Ratcliff and Shadwell were the setting for Charles Lowder's work). St Katharine's was at the centre of a new ecclesiastical parish containing up to10,000 'souls'- too many for the existing churches to cope with. The response from Chislehurst and the surrounding district was phenomenal for within two months the fund had reached £2,100 with only another £900 to be found for the first stage.[10] The Rev. T.C. Johnson had been put in charge as Curate and started his work by providing mission services in the Board School and also, for evening services, back in his previous Parish of Camberwell: how the Rotherhithe people reached Camberwell for evening services is not explained. If it was on foot it would seem that the new Church of England presence was indeed welcome. On the first Sunday 160 children came in the morning and 250 in the afternoon.

Johnson made a plea in the St Nicholas' Parish Magazine for Chislehurst volunteers to act as district visitors or as lay helpers. He could see so much that needed to be done and such enthusiasm from the people but had neither sufficient space nor manpower. An important point was that in the new church one evil of the past would not be perpetuated: 'The appropriation of seats in past times has been a chief cause of the Church having so largely lost its hold of the working classes. We should quite fail, and deserve to fail, if our seats were not *entirely free*'.

The church was not given the name St Helena because of the area's previous bad reputation as a 'rough ungodly' sort of place and where St Katharine's was built was eventually named Eugenia Road – a tribute to the Empress? FHM made clear to his congregation that, as well as raising money for the building of the Church and Mission Rooms, he wanted 'to promote an active and continued interest in the work of the district now and in the years to come'. By June of 1883 three Chislehurst ladies had undertaken to give one day of each week to district visiting and a group of Chislehurst people had guaranteed the stipend of a full-time Mission Woman. The donations from Chislehurst people were all the more praiseworthy because the start of the St Katharine's project coincided with yet another demand on their purses – urgent repairs to the Village Hall. Then there was a plea from St Katharine's for help with financing a children's Sunday School outing: with 500 children on their books it was going to be a costly 'do'. The response was surely more lavish than envisaged when the request was made: the Parish Magazine reported that 'Mr Hoare most generously and liberally provided a tea for 430 children and their teachers who had come for a day's outing from the district which Chislehurst had taken under its care'. However, the people of Chislehurst must have wondered when they would ever be free of subscription demands: underneath the item about Mr Hoare's tea party there was a call from St Peter's, London Docks, suggesting subscriptions of one penny a week, to be paid quarterly in advance. Collectors were needed.

In July 1883, when the Rotherhithe project was only six months old and there was as yet no church nor ancillary buildings, the attendance at services was quite overwhelming and Johnson decided to hire a large tent capable of holding 230 persons. This, obviously, had to be a temporary measure but there was tangible evidence that bricks and mortar were soon to be forthcoming in that the Rector officially laid the foundation stone of the proposed Parish Room on the 28th July. The inscribed stone marking the ceremony can still be seen. Building completion was expected by October. As it turned out, with extra workers employed, the first services were held on the 30th September. Chislehurst and its neighbourhood had by then subscribed £4,000 and so the Bishop's Ten Churches Fund was empowered to give a grant of a further £4,000, to be available as soon as the building of the church had started. The church was due to be finished at the end of September 1884 but sadly, because of expense, the idea of a tower and bells had to be abandoned. Unlike the Church of the Annunciation, St Katharine's never achieved its tower.

The Rev. T.C. Johnson must have been an outstanding organiser. Where he had not enough space he hired other accommodation – not wanting to lose those who turned up so enthusiastically in the early days. As well as the Sunday Schools there were Mothers' Meetings (they also had a day out in Chislehurst), a Band of Hope, a Cricket Club and a Boys' Club, with plans for a Lending Library: all this within the first twelve months.

The church was consecrated on 18th October of the next year, 1884: that it should be ready to time was a miracle because the architect, W.O. Milne, had to grapple with many problems, not least the treacherous nature of the ground itself. A surviving photograph reveals the impossible alignment of the pews on the south side. The style was Early English with a block brick exterior and an interior of red brick with white stone dressings. The altar was raised ten steps above the level of the floor and on it there were six tall candlesticks. Owing to the generosity of donors the church was richly equipped with all the ornaments thought necessary for a ritualistic church. In 1896 St Katharine's was presented with the East window and altar from St Nicholas' Church whose chancel was extended to celebrate the jubilee of the Rector who was, by this time, 'Canon' Murray.

Unfortunately, the church was almost entirely destroyed by a bomb in the Second World War and has been rebuilt in a very practical style: the new church is constructed on the deep foundations of the original.

In 1884, when the new church in Rotherhithe was triumphantly making its presence felt, FHM summed up his vision in a letter to his Chislehurst parishioners: 'One great object I had in proposing this subject to you was that we should take up

ST KATHARINE'S ROTHERHITHE.
W. O. Milne, Archt. Cost, £. 8,000.

some such needy district and "out of our abundance supply their want", and so both find an outlet for energy amongst the teeming needs of such a population . . . and do something to bind together class with class, and suburban parishes with parishes in London'. Indeed, Chislehurst worked and gave in abundance. Mrs Charrington, wife of a churchwarden, was horrified by what she saw of the lives of the inhabitants of Rotherhithe and put out an eloquent plea for cast off clothing and linen. One response here was a regular working party at Miss Campbell's where clothes were made for the poor. However, Mr Hankey of Bickley thought that the problem was basically one of over-population and suggested that something should be done about organising celibate life amongst the labouring classes. He proposed that this should be achieved through addresses from the pulpit.

The Parish Magazine bubbles with accounts of activity and success at St Katharine's, how 'bright religion supplies the longing for beauty in the souls of the poor in their dreary surroundings'.[11] For a few years the Chislehurst Parish Magazine was officially named on the cover as 'Chislehurst and St Katharine's, Rotherhithe, Parish Magazine'. In addition, the Mission Church of St John the Baptist had been set up in Chislehurst in 1886 and that also had a section in the Parish Magazine.

By 1888 the Vicarage was complete and the demands on the Rev. T.C. Johnson, with insufficient staff, were hardly bearable. He put in a plea with very much force for 'the *continuance* of the interest which Chislehurst has always shown which seems in danger of languishing now that church and vicarage are built'. In 1890 the Rector wrote in the Parish Magazine of his regret that 'so little real help is given now from this parish . . . the interest once felt has gradually declined'. He wished to 'make the connection between the two churches more real than it is at present' by more attendance at St Katharine's services.

The story of St Katharine's must not end on a down beat. For FHM, the founding of St Katharine's was the equivalent of Charles Lowder's formation of St Peter's, London Docks. The area was very similar, being the source of labour for the Surrey Docks. The congregation in Chislehurst, by normal standards of church to church generosity, continued with magnificent support well into the next century but the effort of visiting the church and helping with the good works was understandably not maintained. Now, the support for St Katharine's is at the level of greenery at Christmas and the occasional donation. One of the besetting problems of the area has always been, and still is, the shifting population: it is difficult to find lay people who can devote themselves to church activities.

Over the years 1899-1900 the Rev. T.C. Johnson found that the toll on his health was too great: he was exhausted by the effort of putting life into a new church where, just as at St Peter's, London Docks, there were two jobs to be done – ministering to the growing body of people within the church and winning over the never-diminishing body of people outside the church. His place was taken by his assistant, the Rev. E.M. O'Hara Lee, a greatly loved priest who vigorously continued the expansion and influence of St Katharine's.

Death of Mrs Murray

Mrs Murray, wife of the Rector for thirty-four years, died in 1888 at the age of sixty-six. Such an event with the inevitable tributes and acknowledgements in the Parish Magazine and local papers reveals the high regard in which the Murray family was held. Francis and Mary Murray were greatly loved: the sorrow at the loss of Mary and the sympathy for the Rector were equally profound. The Rector could not reply to the great number of letters he received. Mary had devoted herself to the service of Chislehurst not only by her support as Rector's wife but also by active involvement in village affairs: the Mothers' Meeting was her special concern and she carried on long after her condition was known to be terminal. She was a welcome visitor to the homes of the poor and was well known for hospitality on a grand scale at the Rectory. The funeral was conducted by Bishop Jenner: there was a procession of twenty-seven clergy, a full choir, at least eighty mourners, and representatives of every family in the village. Extra police had to be brought in to watch over the crowds on the Common.

The chief mourners were the Rector and Mrs Murray's daughter with her two children.

---

1 E. Lawrence Gee, *The Rich and Poor of Chislehurst 1845-1900*. This study is the source of many of the statistics supplied in this chapter.

2 The following details come from the Minute Books of the Management Committee and the School Log Books.

3 The not-so-subtle system of securing donations to Chislehurst's many projects was to publish the names and amounts of the principal subscribers in the Parish Magazine.

4 Mr Miller was one of the school managers.

5 The Trustees' Minute Book.

6 Mrs Eggleton was the headmistress of the girls' school. Mr Eggleton was not present at managers' meetings.

7 Webb, Miller and Beckwith, *The History of Chislehurst*. In time-honoured fashion the people of Chislehurst were in the habit of fixing their social events on moonlit nights.

8 In the list appears Mr (later Sir) Thomas Firbank MP, the father of the novelist Ronald Firbank (1886-1926) whose childhood was spent in Chislehurst. The family money had been made from the development of the railways.

9 The post-war replacement of the original church can be seen on the right as one approaches London Bridge Station from the south.

10 The subscription list contains many unfamiliar names and there were anonymous donations, great and small. For example: 'Two friends' (£100 each) and 'Mary' (5s). The credit for organising the money-raising goes to one of the curates, The Rev. J.B. Parker.

11 From a talk given by the Wilberforce Missionary in the Rochester Diocese to a gathering in the Chislehurst Drawing Room of Mr Richard Foster, a tireless money raiser for new churches in south London. He was much more responsible for the founding of St Katharine's than is generally recognised.

Chapter 17

The Parish Priest – and more!

It is good if you can maximise collaborative working and team building. But beware: a clear focus and a sharp edge are crucial to this strategy, and it is your authority and your leadership that must provide them. More important than creating formal team 'structures' for consultation . . . is constant communication from the top (yes, you are the top: let's face facts) – to make everyone feel enthusiastically part of the plan.

JEFFREY JOHN, *Going for Growth: a strategy for incumbents of smaller parishes in the central and catholic traditions.*

AFFIRMING CATHOLICISM 2001

By no means was 1890 the 'beginning of the end' for FHM. At seventy years of age, now an Honorary Canon of Canterbury Cathedral, he was in fine health and destined to spend the next twelve years, not 'retired' of course, but reaping the benefits of a conscientious discharge of his duties since 1846. Such was the stability of English life in the latter half of the nineteenth century that there were many residents of Chislehurst who had known but one Rector and one Queen in their whole lives: both Rector and Queen were to provide the excuse for Jubilee celebrations in the 1890s. At one time it had been thought that FHM would succeed to the Dukedom of Atholl but this event was somehow avoided: according to *The Westminster Gazette* the life of a parish priest 'was more to his taste'.[1]

Celebrations, particularly if they involved food, were a feature of Victorian life and Chislehurst was unrivalled in staging village events: indeed, with the Common at the centre of the village 'Merrie England', characterised by travelling fairs, feasting, bellringing and maypole dancing, never died out entirely. A good example of a feast took place well before FHM's time but the tale is worth recounting. The Rev. Francis Wollaston who was Chislehurst's worthy, learned, eccentric Rector (1769-1815) captured the general mood of rejoicing on the signing of the Treaty of Paris and the exile of Napoleon Bonaparte by throwing a great party for all the residents of the village: 1,030 persons in all.[2] On 7th July 1814 trestle tables were laid out on the Common in front of the church while behind them Union Flags fluttered gaily: between the trees were slung banners proclaiming, 'Glory to God', 'Peace on Earth' and 'Goodwill to Men'. The band, on a specially constructed stand, added yet more gaiety to the scene as did also the bellringers with their 'phenomenal peal'. Best of all, the banquet, paid for by the Rector, was brought across from The Tiger's Head.[3] However, by the time Francis Wollaston died in November 1815, Napoleon had made his escape from the island of Elba, suffered defeat at the Battle of Waterloo, surrendered and been exiled a second time, to St Helena. No doubt Wollaston turned

Francis Murray in his last decade

in his grave (on the south side of the church) when the bogeyman's nephew, the exiled Emperor Napoleon III, was welcomed to make his home in Chislehurst in 1871.

The villagers must have been delighted when after thirty-one years of Dr Dawson, the rather half-hearted incumbent who succeeded Wollaston, there arrived the handsome young Francis Murray, son of their Bishop. The fact that he brought his charming new wife, Fanny, must have had the villagers agog with interest.

They were not disappointed for the transformation started immediately, the first three years culminating in a bright open church with an additional south aisle. In April 1849 the achievements were celebrated by eating and drinking for all. As a start the policemen were given a dinner and FHM gave £1 for buns for the children. On the day of the consecration of the church, dinners were provided for the inhabitants at the National School Rooms and 'it was resolved to supply the families of the poor with bread and meat at their homes'. The cost for this seems to have come from a central fund but 'an expense of about £10 had been incurred beyond the estimated cost'. 'Ladies and Gentlemen' were invited to make additional contributions. There at the top of the list was 'Rev. Murray' with £1.11.0 and the rest duly followed.[4]

Once the Parish Magazine had started in 1867 there appeared lively accounts of the Annual Dedication Festivals with their inevitable feasts (Chapter 11). There was also an account of the rejoicing for the wedding of Mrs Murray's daughter in September 1871: the Rector made sure that there was a share for everyone. No sooner had the happy couple left for a honeymoon at the Anderdon family seat near Taunton than, at three o'clock, the school children and twenty boys from the orphanage were treated to a dinner in the Village Hall – hot meat and pudding – paid for by the Rector. The bellringers and other friends were also treated by the Rector to a dinner at The Tiger's Head.

These generous occasions indicate the almost feudal relationship that bound the villagers to their Rector: that he was personally well-loved and respected by all levels of society goes without question. But indeed, there *were* levels of society and FHM moved effortlessly between them: he had been welcomed by the Imperial family at Camden House and equally, 'by the poor of the parish he was idolised'.[5] Dorothy McCall, in *A Patchwork of Chislehurst,* gives many instances of his kindness: the concern of his servants that he should have only minimum change in his pockets lest he should give it all away; his day-long protection of an old woman at the fair whose coconut shy was under threat from a group of rough men; his decision to spend the night uncomfortably in the summer-house rather than disturb the servants on his late arrival home from London.

There are many snippets in the Parish Magazine which hint at the popularity of the Rector. In 1890 the choir had its outing to Hastings and watched the last part of the match between the Australians and the South of England: ' . . . a happier party of friends never spent such a day at Hastings but we sadly missed the Rector, as we do on all occasions, and we hope that he will be with us next year'.

* * *

Victorian clergymen had many advantages over their present-day counterparts: FHM makes a good model for comparison. He would have spent a lot of time walking between the Rectory, the Church, the schools and the principal houses of Chislehurst. Not only was this good for his health but also it provided the opportunity for casual conversations with parishioners. We know that there were many unmarried clergy (such as Charles Lowder) but most were paired with a good and faithful wife who rightly earned the title 'unpaid curate'. FHM was always supported by a team of women in his house, not only running the household but also active in the schools and other village organisations. Soon after Mrs Murray died two of the Rector's elderly nieces, Lady Augusta Pratt and Lady Eleanor Pratt, came to live at the Rectory from where they ministered to the parishioners' needs. This included passing on their embroidery skills to the schoolgirls.

In addition FHM could share many of the parish chores with his curates, always one and often two of them. The value of these young members of the Rector's team must not be underestimated: whether playing in village cricket matches, accompanying choir outings, organising the Workmen's Club[6] or preaching sermons they were a precious leaven of university-educated men. There was one occasion in 1890 when FHM had to bail out one of his curates who had managed to offend in the Sunday sermon: it had been understood that the Curate had labelled all coachmen and gardeners as being generally dishonest towards their employers. So much indignation had been expressed that an explanation had to be put prominently in the Parish Magazine.

This incident illustrates another of FHM's management techniques: he made full use of the Parish Magazine in order to keep people fully informed. Through the Magazine he communicated church notices; he admonished, encouraged and praised; he prepared the congregation for changes in the service pattern and took soundings from those who had an opinion. He used the Magazine to comment on national events, both religious and secular, and such was the tone of authority that it seemed he spoke for Chislehurst itself. His use of the Parish Magazine provided the bonus of allowing him to speak to those who did not normally attend church, or to those who could not attend church because of illness – even to those who no longer lived in Chislehurst but continued their subscriptions to the Magazine.

There was an occasion in 1876 when the Rector was called upon publicly, through the pages of the Parish Magazine, to pass judgement on a controversial matter. Departing from their usual good taste, the amateur dramatics group had chosen two plays which raised the eyebrows of the Editor of the Magazine (this was not the Rector). 'It cannot improve the tone of society to represent either profligacy in high life or dishonesty downstairs as a subject for merriment or ridicule.' Irate at the criticism, seven members of the cast addressed an open letter to the Rector pointing out that the same play had been performed five or six years previously: on that occasion, one of the curates had been prompter and, they added, 'we believe you were yourself present'. In the first instance the Churchwarden, Mr Janson, replied with the observation that a village production was in the nature of private theatricals for a limited group of people and ought therefore to be above reproach. He objected to the fact that 'great fun was made of the deliberate violation of two great social canons: honesty to employers and fidelity in love'. A 'Spectator' confirmed that these same criticisms had been made by many members of the audience and, apropos of the Rector's attendance at the previous performance, the offending parts had, on that occasion, been excised. FHM finally rejoined with tactful praise of the merits of the performers and a hope for 'improved moral perception'. Although the play provided its own moral there was 'often great danger of more attention being paid to the evil than to the punishment'.

The case of the offending play raises the issue of the FHM's own leisure pursuits. His obituarist in *The Westminster Gazette* wrote 'He was a singularly well-read man and a good conversationalist with a keen sense of humour'. Yet neither his writings nor his sermons betray any knowledge of literature, and there are no allusions even to well-known works. The Rule of the SSC to which FHM submitted specified that 'members should avoid all theatres, balls, cards and any public amusements except music, in which there was nothing immoral'.

An important intellectual matter which escaped mention was Darwin's *The Origin of Species* (1859). It predated the Parish Magazine but it is interesting that there was no coverage of *The Origin of Species* in *The Bromley Record*: this indicates that the immediate furore, epitomised dramatically by the British Association debate[7] in Oxford in 1860, caused little or no agitation at local level.

Happily, FHM's self-discipline over food in no way diminished his wish to see others enjoying the conviviality of village junketings but this naturally invites speculation about his attitude to alcohol. The only evidence on the matter is his plea for the formation of a branch of the Church of England Temperance Society which had existed under various guises from about 1830 but was fully established in 1873. The first mention in the Parish Magazine was in September 1875 when a meeting was held in the Village Hall. This consisted of recitations, songs and dialogues bearing upon the evils of drink and the virtue of abstinence. The report is honest enough to comment that 'the meeting was miserably attended but we trust that the matter will not fall to the ground and that some parochial organisation may be formed to grapple with the great giant intemperance which is committing such havoc in our large towns and little country villages'. Temperance Societies promoted either the taking of the 'pledge', perhaps for a limited time, or a promise to be abstemious in general over alcohol. The Chislehurst branch of the Temperance Society soon became quite a lively affair with thirty-three signed up members, FHM being on the committee. The aim was to reduce the dependence upon the public houses and to provide coffee taverns instead. One such venture was established in Chislehurst: the first step in that direction was a coffee and cocoa barrow, donated by a lady in the parish, so that working men could have a non-alcoholic drink either early in the morning or on their way home.

* * *

Finding fault with FHM is difficult: if there were more to say the following two points would not be worth mentioning. Firstly, many of his letters display a somewhat self-justifying tone wrapped up in a rather ingratiating style. In Chapter 6, as a member of the *Hymns Ancient and Modern* committee with its frequent need to 'pour oil on troubled waters', his placatory ways were useful: no doubt the same style was effective when in trouble with the Archbishop.

The other criticism is more serious: in Chapter 14 we saw his capitulation over *The Priest in Absolution*. But for a couple of months, he would have been a founder member of the SSC and had been an active contributor and supporter for more than twenty years. For those twenty years all of his closest clergy friends, including his Curates, had been members of the SSC and so his immediate rejection of the book and hasty withdrawal from the Society seem, at this distance, close to betrayal. No doubt his resignation was inevitable, given the pressure from his congregation, but a few more liberal words about the book from such a respected figure would have added balance to the discussion. It would have been impressive if he could have spoken, or written, more fervently on the principles of the SSC and his belief in its aims. However, in his defence, it could be that he was gradually tiring of the SSC as new blood came in, more liable to be controversial and not necessarily as disciplined as in former times. He was now finding himself outvoted on his propositions and he certainly had doubts about the more Roman aspects of the organisation.

* * *

Having withdrawn from the SSC in 1877 he remained involved with many projects. For some time he had been an enthusiastic promoter of *Archaeologia Cantiana*, an academic periodical which set out to explore the history of Kent, and continues to do so. Back in 1857 he had been involved with the projected publication of a handbook to the locality: this I have not been able to track down (perhaps it never materialised) but there remains a letter from FHM to Sir John Lubbock. In the letter he apologises for his own dilatoriness and reminds Sir John of his offer to write about 'Keston, Knockholt, Chelsfield, Well Hill and the valley of the Cray as far as Bexley'.

The high point of his interest in local history was the publication in 1899 of *The History of Chislehurst*. There were many contributors but the principal editors were E.A. Webb, G.W. Miller and J. Beckwith. The frontispiece is the photograph of FHM shown in this chapter and the Preface states that the history 'was undertaken at the request of the Rev. Canon Murray who had already collected materials with a like purpose'. He contributed to the book an account of his personal reminiscences; he also contributed generously to the costs of publication so that the price for purchasers could be kept down. The resulting tome of nearly 500 pages with sixty-four illustrations and maps and pedigrees is scholarly, reliable and thorough, easy to read and also well indexed. It can happily be read right through as an unfolding story or it can be dipped into for specific points. As an example of a village history up to the end of the nineteenth century it can hardly be bettered. As Roy Hopper said in his introduction to the centenary edition, produced by The Chislehurst Society in 1999: 'It can be used to promote or suggest further lines of research, mined for information, questioned and challenged, used as a guide on walks around the village or simply enjoyed as a vivid window on the past'.

Another of FHM's ventures in print was *The Canterbury Diocesan Kalendar* which he edited for many years. He was the ideal person for this mundane but necessary work: it meant that he was perpetually in touch with clergy throughout the Diocese.

Allied to his concern for history and heritage was his care of the churchyard. That it was and is a well-cared-for place owes much to the ideals of FHM, who made clear in the Parish Magazine that the churchyard needed to be governed by good taste, and also by the rules of land management. There was a lot in the early days about the drainage of the churchyard: the fencing was always kept in good repair and FHM ensured the necessary felling of trees. He was very particular about the style of memorial and there is a correspondence in the Archbishop's archives on the matter of two proposed designs, one an obelisk or, as an alternative, 'an ugly square shape'. The controversy caused FHM to claim that he could, as incumbent, ban an undesirable grave stone. However, the Archbishop's legal department advised that the incumbent did not have the right to ban a memorial which was not to his own taste. As FHM had 'for many years vetted the memorials' this was unwelcome news. This incident took place in 1876 and the proposers for the memorial stone, employees of the Whitefriars Glassworks, wished to remember their colleague Mr Golding: he had lived in the parish for many years and was much respected. Searching the list of memorials in *The History of Chislehurst* does not produce a Mr Golding so we must assume that FHM put up enough objections for the plan to be abandoned.

Looking for a moment at the interior of the church there was one development in which FHM may well have erred. Influenced no doubt by his continental travels he seems to have had a penchant for wall-paintings. These are very successful at the Church of the Annunciation but those in St Nicholas' Church have now been removed. They were certainly there in 1866 and 1899 but had the effect of making the church appear smaller and overpowered.

That FHM loved foreign travel is mentioned by more than one obituarist: he is declared to have been at his best on holiday excursions and, what is more, he made the most of his experiences by giving illustrated lectures in the Village Hall on winter evenings. For example, the Catacombs of Rome illustrated by lantern slides. But there was another method by which FHM transported his congregation far away from Chislehurst: in the 1890s he welcomed to St Nicholas' Church a succession of exotic Bishops and missionaries from all over the world. With neither television nor radio, nor lavishly illustrated magazines, the visiting preachers provided star entertainment and were accorded an enthusiastic hearing. FHM did not confine his travel to Europe: he certainly went to the United States, Canada and Russia. It may have been that his visit to Canada was to see his younger brother, Sir Herbert Harley Murray, Governor of Newfoundland from 1896-1899.

His adventurous spirit famously took him up in a balloon in 1899 – this was at very nearly eighty years of age and with a heart attack (1896) still on everyone's mind.[8] A balloon was to go up from the Glebe Field in order to raise money for the

Cray Valley Hospital. Eight hundred people paid their money and gathered to watch the balloon take off in the 'capable' hands of Mr Cecil Shadbolt. FHM's inclusion in the passenger list had not been made known to the crowd so there was a gasp of dismay when, wearing his clerical hat and an extra thick woollen cardigan, he climbed into the basket. Starting the ascent proved a problem and during the wait some anxious parishioners clung on to the Rector's coat tails in the hope of pulling him out. Their concern was in fact well justified for things did not go well. Much delayed, Mr Shadbolt decided to loose the ropes and get off the ground in spite of inadequate gas. It is a pity the story does not end here for what could be more appropriate than that FHM, like Elijah, should ascend gloriously to heaven in a whirlwind? More prosaically, the balloon skidded through the air at no very great height, crossed the Thames and eventually came down in a coal yard in Beckton. By now, the Rector's hat had been squashed flat. The brave party suffered a vigorous jostling by a local mob and the coal owner demanded compensation which, after a bit of bargaining, was settled: only then were they released, seemingly none the worse for wear.

* * *

FHM's Jubilee, three years previously in 1896, was a magnificent occasion but must surely have been a hidden strain on a seventy-six year old: indeed it could have precipitated the heart attack which followed soon after for which doctors advised six months of rest. The event consisted of two quiet presentations and one far from quiet celebration on the Common.

Since 1887 FHM had performed the duties of Rural Dean for West Dartford and from the clergy under his care he received an illuminated book inscribed with their names; also a handsome memorial of appreciation listing his qualities of courtesy, his ready sympathy and his generous hospitality. More tangibly he received a pair of silver candlesticks and a silver mounted blotting book.

His recognition from the parishioners was lavish. He must have been overwhelmed by the truly magnificent leather-bound book which was put into his hands. The list of subscribers began with the Archbishop of Canterbury, three Bishops, a Dean and an Archdeacon followed by the Community of St John the Baptist, Clewer; the people of St Peter's, London Docks; the Confraternity of the Good Shepherd at St Peter's; and the Congregation and the Mothers of St Katharine's, Rotherhithe. There then followed the names of hundreds of subscribers from the parishes of St Nicholas' and the Church of the Annunciation together with a fulsome appreciation of all that he had achieved in his fifty years in Chislehurst. The crowning memorial to his work was 'an enlargement of the chancel of that church, which for half a century has been the centre of all your loving work'. (According to the vestry minutes a sum of £1,700 had been raised.) The Rector replied to the speech with due humility, emphasising that all achievements were by God's grace and the happy harmony which prevailed in Chislehurst. There were 1,800 people at this ceremony.

Speeches over, there were many celebratory activities including a gymnastics exhibition and a maypole dance of shepherds and shepherdesses. Finally, there was a fireworks display which included, in letters of fire, 'Canon F.H. Murray, 1846-1896' and 'God bless our Rector'. The Band played the National Anthem as a signal for dispersal.

A selection of village activities, not necessarily supervised personally by the Rector but certainly endorsed by him, will show why there was such a united spirit in Chislehurst and why so many people felt touched by his leadership. The list is culled from the Parish Magazines which suggests that these activities were under the umbrella of the church, however vaguely: the Schools, the Shoe Club, the Clothing Club, the Coal Club, the Blanket Club, the Reward Club, the Work Club, the Organist Fund, the Orphanage. However they were all, at one stage, grouped together as the Chislehurst United Benefit Society of which FHM was a Trustee. Outside Chislehurst, but supported by Chislehurst subscriptions, there were the SPG, the SPCK, the Kent Penitentiary, St Katharine's, Rotherhithe, and St Peter's, London Docks. The Workmen's Club and the Temperance Society have already been mentioned. There were also the Amateur Dramatics, the Literary Society (which sometimes had greater expectations of Chislehurst's intellectual level than was justified) and the Juvenile Missionary Society. Directly under the church's supervision was the administration of the Charities and Bequests, the raising of money for Foreign Missions, the Sunday Schools, the Church Choir (five practices a week), numerous Bible Classes, the collection of monies for the Parish Magazine and the organisation of the School Treats. One charming custom was the presentation of Bibles for 'cleanly and tidy cottages' – the mind boggles at the practicalities of making the awards!

In 1894 FHM was elected to the first Parish Council and attended meetings, almost without fail, until his death in 1902.

* * *

Although his hold over Chislehurst resembled very much that of the landowner and squire, FHM would not recognise himself as such and would contend that he cared for nothing but the great work of Christian worship and teaching. Throughout more than fifty years his building up of the spiritual fabric of Chislehurst had gone hand in hand with the development of the more outward signs of spiritual growth – the new churches, the increased number of services at church and the large attendance. The Lent and Easter devotions of 1899 illustrate the busyness of St Nicholas' Church: the same applied to both St Katharine's and the Church of the Annunciation.

At the beginning of Lent, through the medium of the Parish Magazine, FHM instructed the congregation that the meaning of fasting was 'going without food' and abstinence was 'the deprivation of some particular kind of food'. Fasting could be interpreted as taking only dry bread and a little tea or coffee up to lunch time: fasting Communion was always recommended unless the communicant was too frail.

During Lent there were many opportunities for extra church attendance and there were regular addresses from guest speakers on Tuesdays, Wednesdays and Thursdays as well as Lenten Catechising for the children.

In Holy Week, between Palm Sunday and Easter Day there were at least seventeen services including the customary Three Hours Devotion on Good Friday and a 5pm service in the churchyard on Easter Eve. On Easter Day itself there were Holy Communion Services at 5am, 6am, 7am, 8am and 12.15pm and then, over the next three days there were a further ten services.

* * *

If we imagine the Rector walking backwards and forwards to his church as the century came to a close, slower but amazingly upright to the end of his life, we can only wonder at how many of his friends and family he had survived. He was no stranger to the pain of bereavement: the loss of his first wife after only four years of marriage and the loss of a dear son twenty years later. His second wife Mary had died in 1888 and there was now only one remaining member of the Anderdon family in Chislehurst, Maria. Charles Lowder was dead as were many of FHM's contemporaries in the SSC. These included Bishop Jenner who had spent his childhood in Chislehurst, had been at Harrow with FHM, and who had preached at FHM's Jubilee Service of Thanksgiving. The death of another friend had occurred in 1899: that was Mr George Buchanan Wollaston, grandson of the Rev. Francis Wollaston. Mr Wollaston, an architect and former pupil of Pugin, had been a mainstay of Chislehurst life for forty-six years: he had been Rector's Churchwarden for twelve years and had, without fee, supervised the rebuilding of the church spire after the fire. He also contributed to *The History of Chislehurst.*

FHM's sparring partners, Lord Sydney and the Rev. William Fleming of Christchurch, had also predeceased him.

On the national scene the end of an era was being played out. Gladstone, a great Churchman as well as Prime Minister who had been a frequent visitor to Chislehurst, died in 1898. Archbishop Tait had died in 1882 and there had since been two primates, Edward White Benson and Frederick Temple. Queen Victoria's death at the beginning of 1901 was particularly significant to FHM who wrote long and eloquently of her qualities. The Chislehurst Easter Vestry Meeting composed a letter which spoke of 'their deep sense of loss and their grateful recollection of the great benefits which it [the country] has received during her long and beneficent reign'. FHM received a reply, on behalf of the King, thanking the Vestry for their loyal and dutiful communication.

* * *

FHM's own death came quite suddenly on Saturday 11th October 1902. He had returned from a holiday on 28th September and settled back into his usual routine. On the Friday evening he had written twenty letters and, as was his wont, had finished the day's labours with prayer. It was ascertained that it was while praying that he had collapsed and died. Those close to him at the Rectory comforted themselves on how appropriate this was for it had been observed how great a time he spent in devotions: 'Often and often, while men slept, the Rector was striving with God in prayer for the souls entrusted to his keeping. After laborious work, he knelt in his room at the Rectory, literally for hours, praying and interceding: so those about him are able to tell us'.

The parish was stunned as word spread on the Saturday morning. On the Sunday there was a large gathering for a service in church at which the congregation felt his presence most keenly, particularly as they were read a letter which the Rector had left to be opened after his death. Many parishioners visited the Rectory where his body lay and then, on the Tuesday evening, the simple coffin was brought into church to be 'watched' until the funeral. Throughout the night there was a perpetual coming and going of reverent mourners taking their turn to keep the vigil. Large numbers of people attended the Holy Communion Service at 7.30 on the Wednesday morning and there was a Sung Eucharist at 10.15 which was made bright with festal vestments and music. At noon there was a service for children with an address by one of the Curates. And so the prayer and praise continued until the funeral at 3pm. The officiating clergy were two nephews of the Rector assisted by the parish clergy and the Vicar of the Church of the Annunciation. The Benediction at the grave was given by Canon Frederick Murray, the Rector's brother.

The funeral was simple and hopeful – just as FHM would have wished. The words spelt out around the coffin were '*per crucem ad lucem*'.

---

1 Obituary in *The Westminster Gazette.*

2 This precise figure was given on a wooden tablet which hung in the tower until its destruction in 1857.

3 Details of the scene come from the illustration, unfortunately not acknowledged, in T.A. Bushell, *Imperial Chislehurst.*

4 From a note in the archive of St Nicholas' Church.

5 Obituary in *The Canterbury Diocesan Gazette.*

6 The Rector was President and one of the Curates, the Rev. U.I. Easson, was Hon. Sec. The club was open from 6.30 to 10.30 every night. There was a variety of newspapers and periodicals available and writing materials were provided free. There was also Bagatelle, Cards, Draughts, Chess and Dominoes but no gambling was allowed. The club played sports matches against similar clubs in nearby parishes.

7 The principal speakers were Samuel Wilberforce, Bishop of Oxford at that time, and Thomas Huxley, a staunch supporter of Darwin.

8 The following anecdote came originally from *The Kentish Times* but was discovered and quoted by Dorothy McCall in *A Patchwork of Chislehurst.*

Chapter 18

Epilogue

The text of the Memorial presented to FHM on the occasion of his Jubilee in June, 1896

We whose names are underwritten, being past and present Parishioners of Chislehurst and others who have been privileged to know your good work in this place, beg to offer you our heartfelt congratulations on your having at Whitsuntide last, completed the fiftieth year of your service as Rector of this Parish, and we do so not only because it is in itself an event of rare occurrence, but more especially because of the many blessings, which in God's mercy have been conferred on this Parish by your ministrations.

We cannot forget that fifty years ago when you first came to this place you found a neglected church, cold and infrequent services, and an apathy in religious matters which in these days is happily rare, and that your early efforts to remove abuses and to bring back into the parish a higher degree of spiritual life were sometimes met by opposition. We rejoice, therefore, that now on the completion of your Jubilee you are supported by a United Parish, by young and old, rich and poor, alike anxious to testify their affection and regard, and to acknowledge the great influence for good which the example of your consistent and blameless life, no less than your untiring zeal and devotion to your work, have had upon the religious and social welfare of this place.

We wish to acknowledge with grateful hearts the many spiritual privileges we now enjoy, and owe to your earnestness and devotion; the well-cared for Church and Churchyard, the well-ordered and frequent services, the daily Celebration of the Holy Communion, and the numerous parochial organisations, which have been established by your care and energy. The experience of many of us will recall to them times of sickness, of distress, or of bereavement, when their burden has been lightened by your loving sympathy, your active help or your wise counsel. Many too will trace their spiritual awakening to some word spoken in season, some tender appeal to their better nature, or to the still more effective influence of your own life and character 'Gentle unto all men, apt to teach, patient, in meekness instructing those that oppose themselves'. This is the picture of our beloved Rector that we carry in our hearts.

We wish also to put on record our deep sense of thankfulness for the many good works done in this Parish during these fifty years and due to your initiative and liberality, pre-eminent among which are the restoration and enlargement of the Parish Church, the erection of the District Church of the Annunciation, and of the Mission Church of St John the Baptist.

But while as a watchful and faithful Pastor your first thoughts have ever been for the spiritual welfare of your flock, we wish also to bear loving testimony to the unfailing interest which you have taken in all that concerns the social and temporal welfare of this Parish. Notwithstanding the many claims upon your time and energy you have ever been ready to take a leading and useful part in the local Government of this place, to promote every social movement for the elevation of the people, their recreation and happiness, and to help by your sympathy and liberality the cause of the poor and the distressed.

We venture to express an earnest hope that on your part you have been able to recognize some quickening of the spiritual life among your Parishioners; some response to your continual prayer on their behalf; some lasting fruit of the spiritual elevation and loving earnestness of your pastoral appeals to them, and of your fervent championship of positive religious truth.

It has been our desire to mark by some special memorial, our deep sense of gratitude to Almighty God for these many privileges and blessings, and in furtherance of your own wishes, it has been decided that this Memorial shall take the form of an enlargement and enrichment of the Chancel of that Church, which for half a century has been the centre of all your loving work. We now offer to you this tribute of our gratitude for the Glory of God, in the hope that it may not be only an enduring memorial of your faithful services as Rector of this Parish for the past fifty years but also a lasting witness of the deep respect and affection of your people.

While your work in this Parish must ever be foremost in our minds we do not forget the great services which you have rendered to the Church at large, and the high position which you have attained in her councils as one of the Proctors in Convocation of this Diocese and Dean of this Rural Deanery.

It is our earnest prayer that God in His goodness may long spare you to us in health and vigour of body and mind, to be in the future, as in the past, the spiritual stay and comforter, the father and friend, in the truest sense, of all your people.

Bibliography

Bettenson, H., (ed) *Documents of the Christian Church*
Bradley, A.G., *Our Centenarian Grandfather*
Bradley, I., *Abide With Me: the World of Victorian Hymns*
Bushell, T., *Imperial Chislehurst*
Chadwick, O., *The Victorian Church: Parts 1 and 2*
Chadwick, O., *Victorian Miniature*
Church, R.W., *The Oxford Movement, Twelve Years: 1833-1845*
Dean Hole, *Memories of Dean Hole*
Dictionary of National Biography
Ellsworth, L.E., *Charles Lowder and the Ritualist Movement*
Embry, J., *The Catholic Movement and SSC*
Faber, G., *Oxford Apostles*
Frere, W.H., revised Frost, M., *A Historical Companion to Hymns Ancient and Modern*
Gee, E.L., *The Rich and Poor of Chislehurst: 1845-1900*
Gray, R., *Cardinal Manning*
Hammond, W.O., *Reminiscences of Harrow (The Old Harrovian)*
Harfield, A., *Blandford and the Military*
Hattersley, R., *Blood and Fire - William and Catherine Booth and their Salvation Army*
Keble, J., *Letters of Spiritual Counsel and Guidance*
Keble, J., *The Christian Year*
McCall, D., *A Patchwork of Chislehurst*
Mearns, A., *The Bitter Cry of Outcast London*
Murray, F.H., *A Hymnal for Use in the Village Church*
Newman, J.H., *Apologia pro Vita Sua*
Oakeley, F., *Personal Recollections of Oxford: 1820-1845*
Ogilvie, V., *The English Public School*
Ollard, S.L., *What England owes to the Oxford Movement*
Oxford Dictionary of the Christian Church
Prestige, L., *Pusey*
Reardon, B.M.G., *Religious Thought in the Victorian Age*
Roebuck, P., *From Sammy to Jimmy*
Scott Robertson, W.A., *Chislehurst and its Church (Archaeologia Cantiana)*
Symondson, A., (ed) *The Victorian Crisis of Faith*
Trench, M., *Charles Fuge Lowder*
Tyerman, C., *A History of Harrow School*
Vizetelly, H., *Glances back through Seventy Years*
Wakeman, H.O., *The History of the Church of England*
Walsh, W., *The Secret History of the Oxford Movement*
Webb, Miller and Beckwith, *The History of Chislehurst*
Yates, N., *Anglican Ritualism in Victorian Britain: 1830-1910*
Yates, N., *Francis Henry Murray (Archaeologia Cantiana)*
Yates, N., *Kent and the Oxford Movement*

Anderdon family letters
Hymns Ancient and Modern Archive: Canterbury Press, Norwich
Society of the Holy Cross (SSC) Minutes

INDEX